THE CARTOON CONNECTION

The Cartoon Connection

The Art of Pictorial Humour
as seen by
WILLIAM HEWISON

Elm Tree Books
London

By the same author
TYPES BEHIND THE PRINT
MINDFIRE *(A novel)*

First published in Great Britain in 1977
by Elm Tree Books/Hamish Hamilton Ltd.
90 Great Russell Street
London WC1B 3PT

Book design by William Hewison

Set in Century Schoolbook and Univers
by Filmtype Services Ltd., Scarborough
Printed in Great Britain by
Butler & Tanner Ltd., Frome and London

The author and publishers gratefully acknowledge the following for their kind permission to reproduce copyright drawings in this book: The Albertina Museum, Vienna, for Dürer's 'Hare'; Mark Boxer; Trustees of the Chatsworth Settlement, for Rembrandt's 'River with Sailing Boat' from the Devonshire Collection Chatsworth; *Daily Express*, for Giles cartoon; *Daily Mail*, for MAC cartoon; Walt Disney Productions; *Evening Standard*, for Dickens strips and JAK cartoons; Barry Fantoni; Jules Feiffer; John Murray Ltd for Osbert Lancaster cartoon, from *Liquid Assets*; *The New Yorker* for drawings by Chas. Addams, ©1959, Peter Arno, ©1957, and Whitney Darrow Jr, ©1958 The New Yorker Magazine, Inc; *New York Herald*, for Gustav Verbeek's strip; Hans-Georg Rauch; Mrs James Thurber and Hamish Hamilton Ltd for Thurber cartoon, from *Vintage Thurber*, Volume 1; S.P.A.D.E.M., for Picasso's drypoint 'Salome', © by S.P.A.D.E.M. Paris, 1977. Finally, very special thanks to *Punch* magazine, which most generously allowed the inclusion of all drawings not otherwise acknowledged, and without whose help the project might never have materialised.

Contents

Foreword

Beneath the warm umber sod of Montignac, in south-west France, humour was born. There, in the far Aurignacian days of 20,000 B.C., a squat, hirsute, browless man one morning dipped his stick in a dark rooty liquid, bent straight again, and, on the cave-wall of Lascaux, drew a joke about men running after buffalo.

Thanks to the whim of time and shovel, we can admire that joke today. We can tell it is a cartoon from the style: jerky, crude, maladroit, and daft.

It is not, however, very funny. This is not to impugn the Aurignacian sense of humour, since one may fairly assume that these were a good-natured folk who enjoyed a laugh with the lads, otherwise they would all have been out hitting things over the head instead of staying behind to redecorate their premises with jovial graffiti.

The reason it is not very funny is that it has no caption.

And it has no caption because man had not yet learned to write.

From which we may reasonably infer that the cartoon is a primitive form of humour, and that the written expression of the comic impulse is an immeasurably sophisticated development of it.

22,000 years later, things are pretty much the same.

Not even the cartoonist has changed much. He is still a good-natured simpleton, an artisan of nib and brush, who, foreign to the complex processes of reason and argument, is capable only of putting down one idea at a time, and of expressing that idea in crude pictures. He has large capable, albeit somewhat hairy, hands, and thinks only if forced into a corner by circumstances beyond his control, as most tend to be; if he has to write, he does so with his tongue curling against his upper lip. He does not read much, since the noise disturbs people sitting nearby.

The humorous writer, on the other hand, is in a different class. Tall, articulate, elegant, quizzical, logical, amazingly well-informed, wise in the matter and manner of the world, he is an

'I can fix up your phonograph in a couple of days but we're having a hell of a job getting hold of the dogs right now.'

artist to the tips of those manicured fingers with which he is able to coax from the cold keys those sustained flights of comic inspiration which make strong men gasp and lovely women fawn.

When the two come together in the small world of the humorous magazine, as perforce they must, they are irreconcilable to the point of permanent conflict. Illiterate dummy that he is, the cartoonist sees the printed word as something which conveniently comes in long grey slabs in order to display cartoons to advantage. Nature has not given him the perception to understand that, on the contrary, it is the cartoon which has the auxiliary function, i.e. it is there to decorate the prose.

Usually, though, a working compromise is reached between the two, otherwise magazines would never get published; and that compromise is generally arrived at in a civilised manner. That is why cartoonists and writers invariably have their hands insured: the risk of breaking a working knuckle against a colleague's chin or of having a dissenting boot come down on a typing finger is one which has kept actuaries in the crinkly green since time immemorial.

But generally the modern cartoonist is not so much belligerent as sullen; since knowing one's place is a very different matter from accepting it. The attendant psychic shock comes out in their work: favourite themes are masochistic (beds of nails), escapist (desert islands), and paranoid (psychiatrists' couches).

They also draw Napoleon a lot.

And they want to be Understood: like the downtrodden everywhere, they feel that if only they could effectively communicate the fraught clunks and rattlings of their innermost recesses, then the world would understand, embrace, and praise.

I have no doubt that that is why Hewison has written this enormous book.

Not, of course, that I've read it. I have as little truck as possible with cartoon culture: ephemeral and instantly forgotten, it impinges itself not at all upon the sensitive intelligence. If I had to invent some sort of phrase to commend the ensuing stuff to the reader, I suppose I should say that it was a naïve domestic volume without any breeding, but I think you'll be amused by its presumption.

Alan Coren

Preamble

APART from the capacity to invent bubble-gum, one other thing that divides us from the rest of the animals is the ability to appreciate a joke. When we got rid of that prehensile tail and improved the design of our thumbs we also made the discovery that among the rest of our effects we possessed a funny bone. Or so the zoological scientists tell us. Humour is unique to human beings, they say, and I don't see any reason why I should argue with that even though I am sure that one of Thurber's dogs could turn a neat line in repartee. So we've all become used to the idea that we arrive in the world with humour as part of our standard equipment, and anybody who looks around and notices that a lot of us have been given short measure will have to keep quiet about it, because the one thing we just won't tolerate is being told we have no sense of humour.

I'm not so sure about all this. About the built-in humour, I mean. I've a sneaking feeling that it's something we pick up along the way, something that has more to do with our individual temperament and capacity for learning than anything that is firmly locked in our genes. Humour is a language, and like talking we acquire it through practical experience; put us in the company of clowns and wits and in time we'll be rolling in the aisles with the best of them.

This book is concerned with one small sub-sub-division: drawn humour, the cartoon, and I'd like to argue in the following pages that cartoon humour is particularly reliant on the learning process. I will attempt some sort of analysis of the different kinds of drawn humour even though I know that when you take a butterfly to bits to see how it works you no longer have a butterfly. What I don't intend to write is a massive survey along the lines of 'From

'Do you mind if I shelter from the rain? I am waiting for a friend.'

Cave Painting to Gerald Scarfe'; what I *do* hope to provide is a completely subjective view of pictorial humour as I have discovered it myself both as a cartoonist and as an editor of cartoons in *Punch*. The emphasis will be on the last thirty years or so. I hope that what I have to say will give some insight into the 'how' of cartoons and cartooning, and that the examples I have gathered here, though chosen because they have the qualities that *I* appreciate, will also trigger a similar response from the reader. I know, of course, that some of them will not – but to get an idea why this is so you will have to read on from here. If you want to look only at the cartoons, well that's all right by me. Here's a particularly nice one by Starke to begin with.

'As a matter of fact I've only been here since yesterday – I was appearing in the ship's pantomime.'

Desert Islands. Now why have these loomed so large and so frequently as a subject for cartooning? Why, when it would be reasonable to assume that nothing more could be squeezed out of this wizened husk, does somebody come along and draw out yet another bright drop? Why is this much flogged cliché so fascinating to the toiling cartoonist? It's a mystery to me. I only hope that the psychoanalysts don't set their bifocals in that direction – heaven knows what *they'd* make of it.

'In the name of democracy, welcome! Up to now we've had a one-party system.'

The Case of Crum

A COUPLE of years ago a young chap who used to work for me came back from lunch with the longest shaggy-dog story you can imagine. 'This is a good one,' he said. 'Just your kind,' and then he sat down and proceeded to roll it out.

The television naturalist David Attenborough, it was soon apparent, occupied a prominent role in the tale; he was off on one of those animal projects for the BBC and with his team of technicians and helpmeets he was aboard a small airplane flying over Africa. The lad told the story well – this genre needs a slow unravelling, the correct sprinkling of extraneous details, a careful combing through the shaggy hair – and it must be said that it was with no little skill that he brought Mr Attenborough down over the top of the steaming jungle, skimmed him across a placid lake, landed the plane on a tiny airstrip, and in no time had the whole gang out into the long grass and carefully stalking the object of their mission – two large mammals wallowing in the shallows by the shore. The sun beat down, the cameraman began to sweat, the producer's mascara stung his eyes, Mr Attenborough's knee-caps gleamed. 'Here,' he whispered back to the recordist, 'here, crawl up closer, it's absolutely essential that we don't miss any of their sounds,' and he indicated the two hippos that were now revealed to them, two hippos lying hull-down in the water with only the tops of their heads showing above the surface.

It was at this point in the narrative that I felt a certain presentiment, a fluttering spasm of *déja-vu,* and one that pushed me towards an act both barbaric and unforgivable: I was about to pre-empt the story-teller's pay-off line.

'And as David Attenborough and the sound-man crept to the water's edge,' the lad continued, 'they heard one hippo say to the other . . .'

It was here that I gave him the chop: '"I keep thinking it's Tuesday."'

He said, 'You've heard it! Why didn't you tell me at the beginning?'

'Not heard it,' I replied. '*Saw* it.'

Now the interesting thing about all this is the fact that this shaggy-dog story had been extruded, extrapolated and

There's a strong element of 'double-take' in this Ed Fisher idea. Very neat.

'Of **course** *we invented telephones first – the Russians merely got all the* **credit** *for it!'*

11

ornamented from a small cartoon by Paul Crum originally published in *Punch*. Not only that, but one that had been published way back in 1937.

It is common knowledge of course that similar or even the same ideas will sometimes occur to a couple of cartoonists – that's within the nature of idea-production – but it's clear that this story going the usual rounds and brought back to me was merely a highly encrusted version of that original cartoon. No one, I think, could doubt its paternity. Crum's hippos were alive and well and living in London all those years after their creation, undoubtedly a proof of some kind that an inspired idea can hook into people's imaginations and stay there for quite some time. To my young assistant it was fresh and contemporary; it appealed to his sense of the zany, the off-beat, it was something that slotted into the same bracket occupied by Spike Milligan's Goons and the Monty Python crowd. A very up-to-date, 1970s joke. Yet Paul Crum thought of this idea nearly forty years ago. And it wasn't a one-off job – you'll find that most of his work demonstrates a similar brand of near-surrealism.

'I keep thinking it's Tuesday.'

Crum (whose real name was Roger Pettiward and who used as his 'signature' that curlicue in the water in the hippo cartoon) had his first cartoon accepted for publication in 1936 and all his work over the next few years indicated a man who had taken a delicate hold on cartoon humour and bent it into an unexpected alignment. He did not survive the war but, as we have seen, his work certainly has. Was he therefore a humorist well ahead of his contemporaries, a man before his time? Or was he merely adding another facet to that long tradition of nonsense humour that we find in children's playground rhymes as well as in Edward Lear, Lewis Carroll, and ITMA's Tommy Handley? What he gives us is something to work on, something to jolt us away from our preconceptions about the form of cartoon humour. We have to make the necessary adjustment. A new kink in the pattern takes time to establish itself, to become part of our general subconsciousness, but the techniques and 'code' of this new alignment have to be learned by all of us if we are to recognise further variations when they appear.

When the *Goon Show* exploded on to the air the planners at the BBC reckoned it was an experiment that might last for only one or two series and it is certainly true that its fragmented formula worked against it in the beginning. But two or three years later when Spike Milligan was creating that bizarre set of characters and giving each weekly episode a firm if crazy storyline, the show quickly built up a cult following which eventually grew into a widespread popularity. Each Goon became a household name and on every corner you would find kids doing their Bluebottle impersonations. What we had all done was to learn the language of their machine-turned brand of anarchy. Later on the *Monty Python* TV show silly-walked its way towards popularity in much the same fashion.

Once we've made that necessary adjustment to a new and different kind of humour, in this case the Crum cartoon, is it fair to say that the Hippos/Tuesday idea is, intrinsically, a funny one? I don't think so. Although Crum's hippos are thought to be a modern classic by myself and other practising cartoonists and it is still quoted and re-hashed as a shaggy-dog story, there is also no doubt at all that to many, many people there is not a glimmer of humour in it. (I've shown this cartoon to quite a few audiences and I cannot deny the leaden response it receives more often than not.) And they would be right. Just as I am right. For the plain fact is that humour is solely and completely subjective. You could argue that if ninety-nine people out of a hundred genuinely laughed at a particular joke, then that would prove that the joke was intrinsically and fundamentally funny. My argument would be that what you have in those ninety-nine are ninety-nine people who had been subjected to a whole mass of similar influences, experiences, instructions and knowledge, and that somewhere in this complex but universal programming that joke stimulated the same response-nerves in each and every one of them. Yet time and time again people will say, 'That's not funny' instead of 'That's not funny *to me*'. A failing they will never admit to, and this applies especially to the English, is the possibility that they possess only an elementary sense of humour, or a stunted sense of humour or, dammit, no sense of humour at all. For this reason, we hate to admit that 'we don't see the joke' – we are niggled, sometimes angry when we don't see it; we always blame the joke and not ourselves. There's even a thin wafer of shame present as if we felt we had failed some kind of test. While many people are quite happy to come clean and indicate that they have no genuine response to or appreciation of the visual arts, and many of them, too, will have no qualms about proclaiming that they are tone-deaf and completely unmusical, there are few who would admit that all manufactured humour left them cold. And I don't use 'manufactured' in any pejorative sense but to establish it as a highly developed act of creation.

It seems, then, we believe that a sense of humour comes to us as standard equipment and without it we are not wholly human or complete; it is assumed to be a certain measure of our quality as

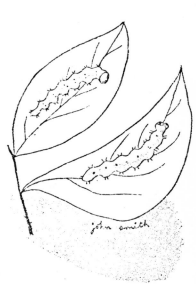

'They'll never get me up in one of those things.'

Here we are at the other end of the biological scale from those hippos across the way but the joke is completely parallel – in fact, its construction and effect are exactly the same: a human spoken cliché shifted into another context. But now there is an extra resonance. We know what the caterpillar does not know – that it will eventually metamorphose into a butterfly and 'get up in one of those things'.

13

civilised persons and the more oblique and esoteric it is the more superior we are. There is some truth in this of course, for after all most of us do tend to move away from the simple pratfalls that had us rolling in the aisles in our childhood as we do from the scatological stories that had us sniggering with the lads on the street corners of our youth. But this improvement (or refinement, if you like) is not one that comes about in the same way as growing taller or developing a bust. There is nothing *natural* about it, rather is it the gradual acquisition of that experience and knowledge I referred to earlier. There's certainly no reason to scorn those people who have not benefited from that experience or knowledge. Which reminds me of the film *Pimpernel Smith* made in 1941 and starring Leslie Howard, in which great play was made of the Germans' complete lack of imagination where humour was concerned. Our Leslie showed them up by reciting Lewis Carroll's 'Jabberwocky' at them, an elegant and supercilious smile bending his lips as the Jerry officers spluttered with incomprehension over 'slithy toves' and 'frumious Bandersnatch'. We were fighting the war of course and this exercise in one-upmanship was reasonable enough in those circumstances, but don't let us believe now that a race or a nation or an individual has a better or worse sense of the sublimely ridiculous. It all depends on how we have been programmed.

But to return to Paul Crum. I think these generalisations I have been making might be clarified if we dug a little deeper and tried to analyse exactly what Crum was doing with his hippos. Of course we might destroy what we already have because there's one certainty in a whole bagful of uncertainties, which is that when you scrutinise and probe the mechanics of a joke it quickly shows itself to be a very delicate construction indeed and will invariably fall apart under your touch. The humorous point released from the drawing acts like a flash of light that illuminates or a quick arrow

As befits the British we never seem to run short of cartoons about dogs. Considering these two it is clear that Scully's derives its quality mainly from the idiomatic caption, whereas David Myers leans heavily on the zany situation and a superbly drawn dog.

'Keeping a friendship in constant repair cuts both ways, you know.'

'You just spoil that dog . . .'

that hits its target; go behind the scenes to find out how it is done and you will never be on the receiving end. Yet let us go against this advice and see what happens.

A cartoon first of all has to feed the viewer with information; the drawing has to be 'read' in very much the same way in which prose is read. Simply or elaborately the ingredients are assembled – the scene is set, the props arranged, the players put in their places. Paul Crum's method was the simple one; those few lines give us all the information we need – the palm trees to indicate the tropics, their reflections to indicate water, those half-heads to indicate hippopotamuses. (Those who don't know what a palm tree or a hippo looks like will already be lost. I'll return to this point later.) Having digested that we then read the caption, which we know from our previous experience with cartoons must be a sentence spoken by one of the hippos. So one hippo is saying, 'I keep thinking it's Tuesday.'

Now why is that funny, at least to some of us? The nearest I can get to an explanation is the one common to most cartoons – expectancy and surprise. When we look at any cartoon we are floated off on a plane of expectancy and anticipation, we are enveloped by the situation as it has been drawn for us – we move through the scenario to that final whip-lash. Reaching the caption our assumptions are turned upside-down; here in the Crum joke the incongruity of a phrase we have often said ourselves is suddenly discovered to be the normal experience of hippos. This astonishing discovery releases in us a glorious spasm of amusement. Or, as someone else once put it, 'the kindly appreciation of the ludicrous'. What we laugh at is not the behaviour of those hippos as animals, but the fact that they are making a pretty good attempt at behav-

'No, it was Edith who ended up as shoes. Alice ended up as handbags.'

'You know, out of all the animal species, I reckon the human must be about the nearest to us in intelligence.'

ing like humans. Humour arises solely out of human behaviour and where animals and objects are the main participants it is their resemblance to human behaviour that supplies the vital thrust.

This 'Assumptions Overturned' formula is common to the great majority of cartoons. Never mind what strange and personal areas are explored by the cartoonist, that basic matrix is one he cannot avoid. If he does avoid it then what he produces is a drawing, a decoration, a light conceit – but not a cartoon. A number of 'cartoonists' get away with this – especially, it seems, on the Continent. These particular excursions into sophisticated whimsy have a bright surface glitter but very little else. What is wrong in these instances is the balance between the idea and its execution; the *idea* must dominate, the *drawing* trail after. For any of us involved in the business of cartooning there is an eternal truth chipped out of granite slabs in letters ten feet high: A POOR IDEA CAN NEVER BE REDEEMED BY A MARVELLOUS DRAWING.

There are, perhaps, other layers to the hippo cartoon, other subliminal echoes – each of us will stand in front of it with slightly (or largely) different mental equipment. That is why, subjectively, it will mean something different to all of us. I can do no more for it than that; I can offer no deep psychological explanations or mind-bending subtleties – that cartoon, that frail construction, is already picked to bits and the broken pieces scattered; doubtless it is hardly funny any more. Dissecting the anatomy of a joke can stop its delicate heart-beat.

So from now on I must tread a little more carefully; no more scalpel work, no more breaking the butterfly on the wheel. Instead I will waffle and ruminate and offer random, if sometimes contentious, observations on the picture material I have gathered together within these pages. Whether these observations open any windows or shed a few glimmers of light on this curious business of cartooning is a question only the reader will be able to answer.

More talking animals. We've even had talking microbes and bacteria, which if nothing else are at least easier to draw.

'I'm getting him conditioned beautifully – every time I run through the maze, he throws me a bit of cheese.'

Watch Out, Here It's Coming

I ONCE went into a church in Tavira in southern Portugal and found an old woman flinging dead gladioli all over the altar and swilling greenish water down a stone channel in the floor. She was not alone; five or six children were chasing a little dog up and down the rows of rush-backed chairs. And through the tall open door and high windows great buttresses of sunlight, solid with dust motes, slanted down and straddled the nave. The dog yapped, the children laughed, the old woman smiled at their antics. All in all, it was a bright, homely place.

Now this I found slightly disconcerting. I had prepared myself before going through that door by adjusting my mood to one of serious respect, carefully composing my expression into that stony solemnity we tend to affect whenever we enter a place of worship. What in fact I found was a children's playground with a high-velocity pooch and a church helper quite happy with the pandemonium. Somehow the frescoes I had come to look at no longer seemed quite so important, because that little church, unbuttoned and relaxed, was dead set against any kind of mystical display and was, for that moment at least, a down-to-earth extension of that bright piece of waste ground just outside the door.

I give this as an example of the way in which we tune ourselves to our expectations, the way in which we assume certain roles to fit particular circumstances. Another less obvious example would be the way in which we rearrange our mental attitudes when confronted with the prospect of humour. Has it ever occurred to you that a joke is really not a joke if it happens to catch us off our guard?

Here is a good example of the customary method with a strip: a succession of similarities followed by a flick in the tail.

I need a man on the Board and we have a number of people here who would fill the position very well.

First of all, Carvington, domineering and a born leader of men ...

... then Barnwell, forceful, aggressive, likes to make his own decisions ...

... also Newton, progressive, blunt and straight to the point ...

18

Receptiveness is all. But given due warning we can field the gag quite nippily and chortle with the rest.

Consider a 'live' audience at a broadcast comedy show – in this case we have a rather gristly example of what can happen when these mental adjustments are taken to the extreme. Instead of behaving like the gathering of individuals they are, these people seem to surrender themselves completely to the corporate whole, binding themselves together in order to make a highly receptive sounding-board for all those drolleries lobbed at them by the performers. The show is meant to be a funny one, and those fellows on the stage are comedians, so the audience sits there brimful with laughter and ready to spill it out at the slightest provocation. I have even heard a studio audience laugh at a line delivered by a comedian in a certain cadence and with a certain pause – a line that *sounded* like a pay-off line but was, in fact, a bit of extraneous padding. The wrong trigger had been pulled but the laughter burst out all the same. The comedian was surprised but grateful; laughs are welcome no matter how they come. That studio audience for its part had been determined to act out its role to the full – it was there to provide laughs and provide them it certainly would.

But for the rest of us sitting at home with only the cat to monitor our reaction things are generally very different. We switch on the set, already prepared, expectant, our mood warmly adjusted. Nevertheless we are still determined to feel the quality and not be conned about the width. That is the difference between us at home and those corralled in the television studio. I admit that studio audiences are fair old game, everybody has a go at them (none of *our* friends, of course, have ever been part of one). All I am suggesting is that they are not even an instance of that subjective appreciation of humour I referred to earlier. To respond to comedy is a pleasurable experience but it is even more pleasurable, apparently, when that response is seen to be shared. In a crowd we are stimulated by the enjoyment shown by the rest of us. To discover

'You are Arthur Goosebender, and I claim my five months' arrears of alimony . . .'

. . . and then Fenshawe, ambitious, likes responsibility, not easily influenced by others.

It's going to be a difficult choice, but I know which man to pick, so . . .

. . .'Congratulations, Grobley.'

19

Two completely different styles of drawing, each absolutely right for its own kind of idea. Saxon — elegant and fluent and very Manhattan; Honeysett — spikey and spidery and very Bermondsey.

'Just when you think you can relax, there's Fra Angelico.'

that we are surrounded by kindred souls whose appreciation of these subtleties is not dissimilar to our own can put an extra gloss on our enjoyment, and the more esoteric the wit, the more aggressive is our laughter, for we are anxious to show those kindred souls that we are no slouches when it comes to the intellectual stuff. Snobbery, of a kind, has poked its nose in.

There is the opposite occasion, of course, when we sit stone-faced in the midst of a crowd of cackling idiots and wonder what they find so funny. The shades of Stephen Potter and his Lifemanship are beckoning, because not only do we want to make it absolutely clear that we have a Sense of Humour but we wish to demonstrate (through nothing stronger than hints, of course) that our sense of humour is of the elevated kind, a sense acutely responsive to the oblique allusion, the piece of well-honed wit, the cerebral satire. Let me give you an example of the sort of thing I mean, an example from some years back when the American Sick Joke was stalking the land. It is a masterpiece of brevity yet absolutely comprehen-

'Here he comes, trying to raise the rent again.'

sive with its information. Its form is a mere snatch of conversation, thus: 'Apart from that, Mrs Lincoln, how did you enjoy the play?'

Neat, compact, everything there you need. The key phrase is *Mrs Lincoln,* which signals *President Lincoln's wife. How did you enjoy the play?* gives us the locale and the situation. *Then* we hop back to the first phrase – *Apart from that* – which we have taken in and stored; but only now do we plumb its full significance. Of course, if we are ignorant about certain facts we can get nowhere near the joke; we must have the common knowledge that President Lincoln was assassinated and that it happened when he and his wife were at the theatre watching a play. All these facts are encapsulated in the one word *that.* If we are aware of all these we quickly get the point.

What I have noticed about the response to this joke is that the laughter is *slightly* louder, *slightly* longer than it ought to be. A small cryptogram has been solved, a test passed successfully, and by Jove they mean you to know it. In this respect cartoons are very different. Cartoons are very much a long distance communication between the joke-maker and the recipient – only two people, the cartoonist and the reader, through the medium of a drawing on a printed page. The reader is on his own. No audience looks over his shoulder to infect him with its merry mood, no performer puts on a funny voice and waits for his reaction. He turns the page and there it is and it's entirely up to him; if he is ignorant about some of the elements in the drawing no one will know – if he is slow-witted he can take as much time as he likes over it. And if he gets the joke straight away and thoroughly enjoys it, few will be aware of it, for it seems to be the general case that cartoons seldom provoke outright laughter. Instead, there is usually an inward appreciation, a hidden salute to that person out there who thought up the idea and drew it, someone revealed only in his signature and the curious way he draws noses.

Another characteristic of cartoon humour is that it is not

'What's a transvestite, mom?'

ruminative, not slow-building to a climax, not fizzing through a series of quips to a quiet ending; its little explosion has been primed on a very short fuse. On this point I doubt whether any single-drawing cartoon needs more than five seconds to do its work – many do it in half that time – but even on the shortest fuse the cartoonist will make sure that we see it burning, then delay the impact until the last possible moment.

The cartoonist is something of a double-bluffer. For his work to succeed at all he must first cheat us, then surprise us with the truth. There is one excellent example of this formula, one that I don't think can be bettered; it is by Bernard Handelsman. As you see, the fuse burns steadily while we take in what we believe to be the situation and while we read the boy's question. The explosion comes only on that final word. Re-phrase the caption to, 'Mom, what's a transvestite?' and the impact is severely muffled. Handelsman, who is a very adroit practitioner of the craft, would never have made that mistake.

'It leaves me speechless – I've only just had that hand-brake adjusted.'

A very different situation is shown in Norman Thelwell's cartoon, but the method is exactly the same as Handelsman's – set it up, then knock it down. You will notice that he underplays the tyre marks and faint ripples in the water of that 'beautiful view' – we come back and notice them only after we have been sent there by those last three words. Thelwell is an extremely competent draughtsman so he is able to meet the demands of his idea; if he had not been able to render this attractive and picturesque landscape the cartoon would not have reached first base. That landscape is the 'cheating' element imperative to the joke. Naturally enough most cartoonists work within their technical limitations, which is a blessing because it results in a wide range of drawing styles – some inevitably more mannered than others. (Several cartoonists hang their style on large noses which means that they are never able to make a joke about large noses; however, as Cyrano has said all there is to say on that subject the loss is no great one.) To return to Handelsman and Thelwell – if we, as

'This is what the church has needed for centuries! A Patron Saint of Dodging!'

To Bill Tidy, drawing is like writing – the images flow on to the paper apparently with very little effort. No subject or theme seems impossible to him – he will tackle a Genghis Khan horde or the *Hindenburg* disaster as if that were the easiest task imaginable. He is a natural draughtsman (luckily for him, untrained) and has packed away in his memory an enormous store of visual information. When many other graphic artists run to their massive reference files, Bill Tidy merely reaches for his pen. His style is robust and inelegant but exactly right for his kind of humour.

'Ten years ago, he'd have seen that coming.'

'Get in, Belshaw! My God, spy exchanges are becoming a costly business.'

'I'm all for exercise, Francis, but they're gabbling the chant!'

readers, hadn't this propensity for jumping to (wrong) conclusions neither of these ideas nor any to the same formula would ever work. This genre relies heavily on that little homily: Things are not always what they seem.

Let me back-track even further to the *Mrs Lincoln* joke. The cartoon by J. W. Taylor has a similar framework and the same brand of urbanity, yet it is quite original. Like the two cartoons by Handelsman and Thelwell, this is a beautifully crafted job. When 'reading' the drawing we notice the black mourning-patch which

*'To be fair, there were no **other** side-effects.'*

we store and then return to only after we have taken in the significance of *no other side-effects,* particularly the emphasised *other*. Taylor could have muffed it by making the caption, *Yes, the tablets my husband was taking had an unfortunate side-effect,* which would have been passable but too obvious. The caption he *did* write approaches at a much finer angle and moves the allusion one step further away. And that *To be fair* is an extra bonus. Underlying the joke itself there is something else, of course – a wry comment on the pharmaceutical industry and all its doings. Taylor himself has therefore made certain assumptions about the readers he wishes to reach (in this case, readers of *Punch*); he expects them to recognise a mourning-patch and the medical use of 'side-effects'. He also expects them to prefer the oblique.

So all three cartoons – by Handelsman, Thelwell, and J. W. Taylor – are to my mind top-quality material, not just for their basic ideas but because of the skill by which these ideas are illuminated. Another part of the skill is that they make it look easy.

It is possible, of course, that those three cartoonists might be very wary of looking at their own work in this analytical way, might even dismiss the process as being rather over-blown and altogether too serious and earnest. But even they would admit, I'm sure, that inspiration and intuitiveness are not the only elements that go into the making of a cartoon. Like most humour this form depends on a collaboration with its audience – the 'language' used has to be understood by both sides – and in the higher forms of the

Any joke to do with illness or doctors rings a bell with most of us because it deals in a familiar area of anxiety: not quite whistling in the dark but something like that.

craft it relies more and more on suggestion, implication, and allusion. There is a kind of assumed agreement between the joke-maker and the joke-receiver; the one presents a riddle and the other makes an effort to solve it. So we get hints rather than flat statements, implication instead of explication, and deliberate blanks for the reader to fill in himself – all of which heighten the degree of pleasure we get when the riddle is solved.

How do we assimilate this 'language'? Only by looking at cartoons, many cartoons, and naturally enough this learning process applies particularly to the cartoonists themselves. What they rest on is the great raft of material that has gone before; they recline on the accumulated output of all those past exponents of drawn humour; their work is derivative in the sense that it is a variation on or an extension of or a reaction against cartoons already done. A cartoonist who had never seen another cartoon would be a very rare bird indeed, an impossible one, in fact. Even those aristocrats of the trade, those few who break away from the mainstream and pioneer fresh territory have had the mainstream to break away from. Steinberg, François, Fougasse, Pont and Crum did not spring fully-armed from the naked soil.

'A word of advice – ease up on the health foods.'

'I don't suppose it's much compared with other inferiority complexes.'

Categories and Divisions

WE'VE looked at the cartoon through the wide-angle lens; perhaps it's time to sidle in a little closer and examine the art in finer detail. When we do, we discover that the general shape I've been suggesting all this time does in fact have several wobbles and kinks in it. The template I've described is true enough, I think, but the patterns cut from it have certain idiosyncrasies, certain departures from the basic form. I'm not referring to differences in drawing style – that goes without saying – but to different categories of pictorial humour. It seems to me that most cartoons fall into one of nine different areas, though I must stress that these divisions are pretty rough and ready and solely of my own making.

The largest sub-division and one that has been with us right from the beginning is Recognition Humour. (I call it that; what the viewer recognises is the workings of human nature.) Then there is Social Comment (quite often Recognition Humour with a Message); Visual Puns (not really jokes but witty sleight-of-hand); Zany (or Screw-ball or Nonsensical); Black Humour (or Sick, or Bad Taste); Satire; Topical (quips about yesterday's news); Faux-Naif (there is also a sub-sub-section which is True Naif masquerading as Faux-Naif); and Geometric (for cartoonists who can't draw but are nifty with the ruler and compasses). A further category could be Strips but really this is a variation of the *form* of the cartoon, not its content.

Of course, there are plenty of maverick styles about which don't fit into any of those compartments and there are some cartoons that manage to spread themselves across two or three, but for our purposes the categories above are all we need to worry about. Only American university students hot-foot after a Ph.D. need to burrow down further in search of the minutiae.

Recognition Humour
Recognition Humour at its most humble level is straightforward

Northerners do go on and on about being so friendly, don't they? So Starke (who, incidentally, was a warm, friendly Scot) was quite in order to give them a twitting. And that 'let fly' is crucial.

'I wish they'd learn that they can't just move into a neighbourhood and let fly with their warm, friendly north-country ways.'

'You were saying something the other day about having lost a skipping-rope . . .'

reportage heightened very slightly by a dash of theatricality; here the cartoonist plucks at our sleeve and points to an ordinary everyday event, and as we are looking he flashes a beam of torchlight at it. The edges become sharper, the shadows darker, the action a little more exaggerated – we see that this very familiar thing is suddenly more significant. The cartoonist has recognised the humour lying just below the surface and by nudging it upwards he has brought it to our notice. And maybe because it's all so familiar and there are no riddles to solve we therefore tend to feel that it's really our own joke, that we ourselves have been involved in creating it. And that, of course, makes us feel rather good.

To be sure of getting that kind of response, the cartoonist must stick very close to the ordinary domestic scene, to Pa, Ma, and the kids, to the kitchen and the living-room, to the back-garden and

Note the man's feigned casual stance, the feigned casualness of the caption, the wide separation of the two main elements in the drawing, the expression on his and her face.

Siggs kept himself pretty close to the domestic scene – only rarely did he go outside it. On the surface his cartoons are humble recognition but you'd be mistaken if you thought they were merely that; they have a strange, lingering resonance, a knack of staying in the mind far longer than you would expect from something so apparently simple. This is why Siggs is much admired by other cartoonists (you might remember these points when you look at the other examples of his work in this book).

'The way she kept on about not minding when Willie broke her precious Wedgwood vase!'

29

the local shops, keeping well within the broadest band of common experience. He must not be literary or oblique or esoteric or even particularly witty, for those elements would make it a different kind of cartoon altogether. It is easy, consequently, for the sophisticated reader to curl his lip over this sort of humour but in doing so he will be deprived of a very real kind of enjoyment. This superior attitude is taken even by some fellow cartoonists, who should know better. Those who ply their pens in the more refined and intellectual reaches of the business can often be caustically dismissive. More fool them, for through his work the humble man is showing that he is a sharp observer of human behaviour and human nature – which is really what humour is all about. He does not direct his torchlight haphazardly; that moment of illumination is very carefully chosen before he presses the switch.

The six cartoons by Graham, Brockbank, Siggs, PAV, Starke and Chon Day are a few examples of the most straightforward recognition humour; from them you can see that the dividing line between describing a fact and describing that fact in such a way as to render it funny is a very narrow one. A hair's breadth on one side and it's funny, a hair's breadth to the other side and it's not.

Now let us consider a selection of drawings that are still recognition, but which overlap and include other facets. The main charac-

'I . . . a woman . . . answered.
She . . . a woman . . . hung up.'

Perhaps not truly recognition for *all* of us, but we've seen it on the pictures, haven't we? The caption has a flavour of American wisecrackery, perhaps because Chon Day is American.

'Why the devil can't you pick a space your own size?'

Most motorists have been in this situation; even Mini drivers have Mopeds to contend with.

'Here comes that damn cloud again.'

I have the feeling that this cartoon will mean more to the British than to anyone else. Our climate is never remote from our thoughts.

'Darling, who is that simply gorgeous man?'

*'Darling, what was the name of your
cousin's border terrier? . . . The one
that was run over by a bus.'*

'Good God! Richard Fearnsley-Smith!'

Graham on his home ground. He has probably got more mileage out of the Cocktail Party subject than any other cartoonist.

teristic note is there still, but permutations of other notes are being added to make up a variety of chords. The three Graham cartoons are from a feature he did for *Punch* on the subject of People at Parties. The first is pure recognition, just tilted on the right side of that dividing line. But extra notes have been added to the other two, particularly the *Richard Fearnsley-Smith* cartoon.

Social Comment
I wrote earlier that Social Comment humour could be described as Recognition with a Message. This implies that it is somehow more worthy than the other category, and therefore better. More worthy, yes, but not necessarily better. Where this humour does gain is in the fact that it is tinged with acid. The joke demonstrates that the cartoonist has a point of view; he looks about him at the passing show (or to put it more pedantically, at the social, political,

and physical scene), notes its movement and direction, and makes his comment. The joke can be a mere flick or it can be a deep thrust, but in either case it makes us look at the subject in a slightly different light than we did before. I'm not suggesting that our own views are then changed, but for a moment we might feel marginally discomforted if the cartoonist's view is not quite our own. On the other hand, if we find ourselves in the same camp as the cartoonist we praise him for being a very funny fellow and one who has his head screwed on the right way. A cartoon about, say, the confrontation between members of the hunt and members of the League Against Cruel Sports will be more or less funny depending on which side of the line we place ourselves, with the cartoonist or against him.

You will see then that in certain instances the social comment drawing can step into the area of the political cartoon, but, unlike the political cartoon, it avoids being declamatory or polemical. It

ffolkes goes many times to mythology and history for his subject matter, but not always. He is a cartoonist who draws the most stylish nudes in the business, as witnessed below.

'I'm afraid of the day when it will seem like just another job.'

*'He **loves** feeding the chickens.'*

sticks to its number one requirement – being humorous. Given all this, I don't think it too far-fetched to claim that the social comment cartoonist is in the way of being something of an historian; he is, after all, a recorder of events, and he reflects a certain attitude to those events. This comes about because he must be continually on the look-out for new material, new areas as grist to his mill, and he is therefore quick to jump at the smallest twist in the pattern as it occurs. It has been remarked that on this score the pages of *Punch* are just as useful a record as many a closely-worked volume of social history.

Again, as in other endeavours, there are pioneers and there are followers; a fair number of cartoonists seem unable to recognise new subject matter when it turns up and they latch on to it only after one of the trail-blazers has presented it in print as a cartoon comment. Once that has happened it is startling how quickly others come up with their own variations. Norman Thelwell has

These are examples of the *real* Thelwell cartoon world: Social Comment with an edge to it.

been such a trail-blazer; he was the first to have a go at the subject of factory-farming but his colleagues were rapidly in on the act once he had shown the way.

The first Thelwell cartoon shown here is quite sharp. Underlying it is a criticism of the battery principle, but there is also a nostalgic note of regret for a departed way of rural life. The second cartoon shows farming as an industry with all those acres of corrugated iron. There's no suggestion of nostalgia anywhere here, but there is an extra layer on that basic acid comment – and that is another poke at farmers' ingrained pessimism. Note again how the 'point' is delayed until the final couple of words. A criticism of Thelwell's work might be that he puts 'cartoon' people into naturalistic and correct settings – but this doesn't worry me; it is these idiosyncrasies that give work its distinctive signature.

'We're still at the mercy of the elements of course – a sudden hailstorm could deafen you.'

Kenneth Mahood has one of the sharpest (and most subtle) minds among the present generation of cartoonists; that his work has appeared regularly in *Punch* and *The New Yorker* for more than twenty years proves a consistent high-level quality. A large proportion of his work falls into the social comment category, but he has also produced many excellent political cartoons. When there was a marked increase in the percentage of foreign cars bought in Britain, Mahood produced a double-spread feature on this subject; the two drawings from that feature shown here are both concerned with the quality and price of the Rolls Royce. Note that the cars are technically correct in detail but they are caricatured to the same extent as the people. Mahood's Father Christmas cartoon is a neat bit of Union-bashing, but he can and often does bash Management just as effectively.

'Damn it, Baker! It's the middle of March – won't the union let him do **anything** *else?'*

'We could have had a Rolls, but who wants a car that only **whispers** that you're filthy rich?'

'If God had wanted this car to be cheap, sir, he would have let the Japanese make it.'

'Would you believe it, Wilkins is the first red-haired left-handed slow bowler to be no-balled twice in the third over of the second day, and incidentally, Bill tells me that is the fiftieth piece of useless information he has given today and his five thousandth of the season . . .'

These pictures were drawn by Pont between 1934 and 1938 and were part of an extremely popular series on The British Character. Forty years on they can still amuse us, yet Pont himself claimed (genuinely?) that he had no sense of humour and that he tried to draw people exactly as they were. It is true that these tableaux stem from a sharp observation of reality but Pont makes them funny by exaggerating what he sees (or rather, what he knows) and then recognising instinctively how far he can safely exaggerate. His is real recognition humour. The drawings themselves are attractive to me because, in spite of their cross-hatchery and careful composition, they are untutored and amateur in the best sense of the word — the work of a natural draughtsman. Pont studied to be an architect (set-square and ruler stuff) but had none of the formal art training which would have shown him that drawing is very *difficult.* So his easy assurance and wiry delicacy of line survived; he was able to tackle subjects that would scare the daylight out of most trained artists, and bring them off beautifully.

TENDENCY TO BE EMBARRASSED BY FOREIGN CURRENCIES ▶

SKILL AT FOREIGN LANGUAGES ▶

THE BRITISH
CHARACTER

◀ THE ATTITUDE TOWARDS FRESH AIR

▲
ADAPTABILITY TO FOREIGN CONDITIONS

◀ FONDNESS FOR TRAVEL

◀ TENDENCY TO KEEP OUT
OF FOREIGN POLITICS

The Fisher cartoon is social comment but with a harder critical edge to it so I suppose it could be labelled 'satire'. All the ingredients are there, clearly stated without fuss, and the reader is left to make the right connections. Ed Fisher is an American cartoonist living in New York but his work has been published regularly over here, particularly in *Punch* and the *Spectator*. The strip by our own David Langdon has a satirical jab at colour prejudice. The humour in this and the Fisher cartoon – even if you can call it humour – is very bitter indeed. Would readers who *are* racially prejudiced have their consciences stirred by these two cartoons? Or is all prejudice so thickly armoured that nothing can dent it? We're still in the same area with the cartoon by Dickinson, though it's a wee bit more oblique than Langdon's and sends out rather more ripples. The prejudiced can perhaps afford to smile at this one because though we rely on the 'Micks' to build our Motorways and Centre Points, and the 'Spades' to run our hospitals and London Transport

'Briggs & Co? You advertise a vacancy. May I call on you for an interview? Thanks.'

Dickinson

– the Irish are not so damn noticeable, are they? Geoffrey Dickinson is one of the few 'artists' who have become cartoonists; he studied painting at the Royal Academy Schools and much of his best work is in colour.

Social comment, then, is a wide-ranging term and because of that it is no surprise that this category is the largest one.

Visual Puns

About twenty years ago it was quite common to come across cartoons that relied on a simple device; what they did was to take a familiar turn of phrase and render it in pictorial terms. The caption of one, I remember, was, 'He has designs on her', and the drawing showed a group of people at a reception where one man was busy drawing doodles all over the dress of a lady guest. Another example was a woman leaning over a pram with a baby in it, saying, 'He has his father's ears'. Yes, you're right, the baby held an ear in each hand.

These were visual puns of a kind, or perhaps they are best described as Visual/Literary Puns. Straightforward visual puns, the kind I'm concerned with here, are rather different. Whereas ordinary puns play around with word associations, the visual pun

DAVID LANGDON

'So sorry, but since you rang,
the vacancy's been filled.'

makes its point through the similarity of one image to another, associations which the cartoonist has been quick to notice and then bring together within the boundaries of one drawing. Literary puns can be many-layered, oblique, and witty when at their best, but on the whole visual puns tend to be fairly simple. Only occasionally are they so neat and telling that they linger in our minds long after our first meeting with them.

This kind of image-linking, of course, is one of the mainstays of poster art. I remember two of Abram Games's posters from the last war in which this technique was used. One was a 'careless talk' poster for use in the Far East; in it the almond-shaped eye on a Japanese face was transformed by Games into a midget submarine. Another was on display in Army units in 1945. Its purpose was to encourage soldiers to use their vote in the General Election and it had Games's usual strong design and stylised imagery, in this instance a vertical column, the top half of which was the Big Ben tower, the bottom half a pencil – and the whole shaft gripped by a hand. I believe the pencil point rested on a drawn X. There would have been a slogan on the poster, too, but I can't recollect it – proof that a good pictorial image is more potent than a string of words.

The use of this visual pun was primarily a symbolic one: Big Ben/Pencil = Parliament/Vote. Cartoon visual images are much more frivolous, of course, though they can (and really should) have an extra allusion or two hovering around in the background.

Now for some examples, and this time I have decided to select one or two drawings of my own from a period some years back when I found myself inclined towards visual punnery. I make no great claims for them as cartoon humour but they have, I believe, an

Two visual puns, the one obvious, the other less so. The puzzles the reader is set are not too difficult.

extra layer that takes them rather further than a bald statement that two things look alike. That tyre-pump dates the first drawing somewhat (they're all worked by foot these days) but its shape and operation are very similar to the plunger box for detonating explosives electrically. What I was hoping for in this drawing was an ambiguity, a coincidence – a quarry explosion happening at the precise moment a man begins to pump up his car tyre. Or a fantasy – has his plunger/detonator action actually caused an explosion? The 'point' is not precise; the reader is left to wonder about it, just as the man in the drawing is wondering. Things are easier in the theatre cartoon. You don't have to imagine the other part of the visual pun – both elements are shown in the drawing. I'm not sure myself whether the toper is attempting to camouflage those two bottles deliberately or whether he put them there by chance.

The third drawing (overleaf) is a bit more complicated because you have to be familiar with Comic Cuts and the like. Who was that unsung comic artist, I wonder, who years ago hit on that little pictograph whereby a character was shown to be asleep by that cloud above his head and within the cloud a log of wood with a saw halfway through it? Stuck there, with no aid from any hand, that saw was shown emitting a string of Zs – the sound of sawing but also the sound of snoring. So the message was: that man below is asleep. (Again, I wonder if it was the same comic artist who first thought of expressing 'Idea' by putting a shining electric-light bulb in that cloud.) These, and other devices, became the standard vocabulary of the penny comics and even nowadays they can crop up in a more refined form in the pages of *The New Yorker*. So this visual pun of mine links the Zs of the American university T-shirts with the snoring Zs of the comic artist, the situation being a boring lecture which allows the pun to be not completely illogical.

'Isn't that our au pair girl?'

This cartoon has an element of 'double-take' about it. We come back to that hat to be sure that it *is* covering her face.

Zany

I once tried to define the adjective *zany* to an anglophile Dutchman and had to give up the task. It seems to be a word that refuses to be pinned down. There is a dictionary definition, of course: the noun *zany* is an assistant clown or buffoon; the adjective *zany* means crazy, clownish. (It derives from the Italian *Giovanni* – which proves once again the zany waywardness of the language.)

It's when we use the word to describe a certain kind of humour that the difficulties arise, for no two people seem able to agree exactly what that is. I tend to recognise zaniness in a cartoon when the idea takes off in a leap of absurdity while remaining anchored to reality by a twist of crazy logic. However, some zany ideas refuse to be tethered in that way but throw themselves into a total anarchy, becoming so personalised that the reader is left to wonder whether the joke is on *him*. Therefore, the reaction to many of these anarchic cartoons is not unlike the cagey, circling attitude many people have towards *avant-garde* art; bemused, suspicious, not wanting to appear gormless but half inclined to feel they're being had, and these difficulties are twice compounded because more often than not the drawings have an arty cast to them and are featured in expensive books. For our purpose here it might be better to stick to that first kind of zaniness I mentioned, the one that is within reach of most of us.

To many people Bill Tidy is the king of cartoonists and I admit it will be difficult not to include too many of his ideas. Although the landscape surrounding professional cartoonists is scattered with fool-proof ideas just waiting to be picked up, ideas that have an inevitability about them, a well-rounded completeness that requires no polish or refinement, none of Tidy's creations could ever fit into this category. The originality of his imagination strikes off on bizarre and exotic tangents and we, the readers, have

'. . . Arsenal lost again, did they?'

to be nimble-footed if we are to follow him; when we do we are rewarded with hilariously funny jokes. If we can't follow him, Tidy would be the first to admit that it is not necessarily our fault, because his method is by its nature a hit-and-miss one, a taking of chances. That the risks come off time and time again places him firmly in that tiny inner circle of grand masters of the trade. We Tidy fans naturally have our own favourite Tidy cartoons; some of the most memorable to me are collected together in a later section.

The Larry cartoon was not one of his *Man in Apron* series, though it could well have been. There were subsequent series: *Man in Office, Man in Hospital, Man in Garden, Man in School* – all composed of quick visual ideas without a caption in sight. (In fact, I cannot remember Larry ever doing a cartoon that needed a caption, though in recent times he has tended to rely on notices and written signs within his drawings.) At his best his jokes can trigger explosive belly laughter – a fairly rare response to cartoons. His real name is Terry Parkes, 'Larry' being a nickname hung on him when he was a schoolteacher, those being the days of Larry Parkes, the American singer who played Al Jolson. It's worth mentioning here that his work demonstrates that perfect marriage between style of idea and style of drawing. Imagine the canary idea drawn by, say, Thelwell or Handelsman, and you will then appreciate how 'wrong' it would be.

In the Taylor cartoon, the unexpected is heightened by the unexpected juxtaposition of different drawing styles. Ken Taylor is a very good illustrator and cartoonist but this example is not only zany but is *near-non-art,* for it relies mainly on neat scissor-work among the engravings in old Victorian books. This approach had a brief flowering in the late 1950s when it allowed people who couldn't draw an opportunity to get in on the act. They had to have ingenuity, of course, and the ability to use a glue-pot and think up a wisecrack (generally the wisecrack had a faint Groucho Marx flavour about it).

In the Heath cartoon, again we find the vital point delayed to the final word in the caption. But I think I am particularly fond of this cartoon because of the drawing. Michael Heath shows time and time again that he has the best visual memory in the business. Others might be just as good on general effects but he surpasses them all with his 'accuracy' of detail. I put 'accuracy' into quotes because the paradox is that the detail is *caricatured* and has not necessarily ever existed. (There are similarities with that other paradox we used to hear in the Life Drawing room: 'Your drawing should be more like the model than the model herself.') Heath is very good on dress (changing fashion) and interiors: it's worth spending a minute or two looking at this drawing, the epitome of that kind of 'twenties/'thirties hotel foyer. I didn't see him tackling this one but I have watched him doing others – a blank sheet, no reference, and straight off with the pen, knitting away until the detailed pattern is complete.

Ken Taylor

'This hotel was always popular with the old stars. Sir Douglas
Fairbanks used to come here and stay in the chandelier.'

This is exactly the kind of cartoon about which other cartoonists groan and say, 'Now why didn't *I* think of that?' It is an idea you feel has been lying around for a long time just waiting to be picked up. And Wiles was adroit enough to pick it up. Fantasy/logic.

'Well, at least we'll be spared watching World War Three.'

This drawing by Heath is taken from a feature he did about the spate of war documentaries being shown on TV; again the details are worth studying – they add up to a sharp account of a certain kind of early 1970s life style.

'It keeps him off the streets.'

This has multiple resonances, but not quite the same kind as Siggs. Eric Burgin was one of the great cartoonists of the 'fifties and 'sixties; he edited himself so rigorously that the number of his submissions to *Punch* was small compared with other 'regular' cartoonists; it was therefore difficult not to accept eveything he sent. Sadly, he died at the age of thirty-nine.

Black Humour (or Sick, or Bad Taste)

I've heard it said that good and bad taste resemble beauty because they, too, rest in the eye of the beholder. I can't agree with that but in a simplistic way I'm prepared to believe that beauty can just sit around there waiting to be recognised whereas taste is something we've got to work at. I suppose that's why the word 'taste' is so often linked with the word 'cultivated'. It occurs to me, too, that there might be another dimension tacked on at the side, which is that taste does not centre itself on an individual but can be said to exist only when it is the accepted attitude of a group. It's a tribal thing. Certainly the decision about whether something is in good or bad taste cannot be made by one person unless his views have already been influenced by his peers. These attitudes form in the group by rubbing off from one person to another, and so on.

When a fastidious dilettante surrounds himself with carefully chosen artifacts in the height of taste, these things can only be in good taste if they are recognised as such by a number of other people, provided these other people are also cast in the same refined mould. If in the course of time a sufficient number of people gang together with the opposite view, then what was originally good taste becomes bad, and vice versa. (Note how those bulbous 1930s' three-piece suites are now so fashionable.)

But what we ought to be concerned about here is the taste in

'I'm cured! I'm cured of my totally illogical belief in religion!'

behaviour, in beliefs, in accepted patterns and codes and the respect owed to these codes. Bring humour into this area and you can be walking on eggs. So certain unwritten embargoes come into being: it is bad taste to make jokes about . . . . . . , fill in the blank yourself. And these are not necessarily important areas such as religion, or sex, or death, or messy violence – a ring can be drawn around patriotism, sacrifice, heroism, physical abnormalities, and even the treatment of animals. (Curiously, the Victorian middle classes, who would have suffered apoplexy over a joke against their Christian religion, were apparently unabashed at the stream of jokes about lunatics and village idiots.) The professional humorist cannot relax and just be his own man, he must recognise that when he sets out his published humour for sale in the market he cannot afford to barge over the line. But, of course, he does. And though his knuckles might be rapped at the time for doing that, his spasm of bad taste effectively pushes that perimeter line a little bit further out. If he makes a self-conscious practice of this, however – going out of his way to shock and dismay – he might no longer be admired as the scourge of hypocrisy he aims to be but will be seen as a little lad baring his backside at his schoolmistress. And I'm not thinking about that kind of humour labelled 'saucy' or 'risqué' or the like – that is mainstream stuff, anyway, the rock base to the whole tradition of music hall humour. No, I mean those delicate areas of deep-felt belief that can be scarified by a bad-taste joke, and particularly when it is an outsider who is doing the scarifying. Somehow gallows humour is more, is perhaps only, acceptable if it comes

YOUR SUPPER'S IN THE OVEN

'The men are bored, Carstairs. I think it's time we had a glorious blunder.'

from one of *us*, one of the believers. Remember that the trench soldier of the Great War had a mordant and bitter and scurrilous wit about his own situation; mutilation by gas and shell was a funny subject so long as the comedian was one of the soldiers, one of the victims. The same joke could not be made safely by a civilian back in Blighty.

Then what about religious jokes? Not jokes about vicars and collection-plates and repairs to the steeple, but jokes about *belief*. Would it be all right, like the soldiers above, if a true believer made a bad-taste joke about that? And is it even then only excusable if it happens to be really funny? (Which means that I have fallen into that old trap – what *is* funny?)

Not long ago a midnight doodler used to keep up a steady supply of felt-pen cartoons on a poster site near my home in Wimbledon and by and large they were pretty good. One day there appeared a drawing of Christ crucified and from his mouth was drawn a speech balloon containing the words, 'What a way to spend Easter'. To an atheist (and possibly to an agnostic) this is very funny. To the practising Christian it is not only in bad taste, it is sacrilegious, too. I'm certain that no magazine or newspaper which is aimed at the general reader could afford to print that cartoon, not in the mid-'seventies, anyway, when all-round circulation is declining without that kind of help. It would affront and hurt a great number of people. Yet who knows, so rapidly are attitudes changing and minds broadening it is possible that similar cartoons to this one might appear in print sooner than we think. (The Fringe and Underground press publish this kind of material already, of course.) After all, we are very much more explicit these days in

Religion and bloody death have not been disregarded by humorists in the past, but what has long been normal in spoken jokes has only recently appeared regularly on the printed page.

cartoons dealing with the broadest area of sex than we were even just a few years ago. The big, glossy 'nude' magazines can now joke about adultery, group sex, pederasts, perverts, even bestiality – and draw it all happening. And even general magazines like *Punch* can now quite happily cartoon sexual intercourse, impotence, and homosexuality (though scatological humour is still given a miss because of its inherent juvenile nature).

In general, then, journals march in step with the main battalions of public taste – sometimes they advance a short distance ahead, sometimes they lag behind, but seldom do they make sorties in all directions. Even so, circumspect as these journals might be, that doesn't stop the flow of letters signed 'Disgusted, Tunbridge Wells', from pouring into their editorial in-trays, and though editors might dismiss them as coming from the lunatic fringe it does indicate that no matter what a paper does some of its customers are liable to be offended. It is amazing what burns people up; if ninety-nine people think something is ridiculous, you can bet there'll be one who believes it to be sacred. Those papers specialising in humour and satire have to take no account of this, of course, and just get on with the job.

Some years ago a cartoonist called Matthias thought up an idea on the subject of guide-dogs for the blind and made it into a quite funny and innocuous little drawing. Or so one would think, yet when it was published about a score of readers thought otherwise and lost no time in getting their letters off to the editor. The blind, apparently, were not a subject for humour; that cartoon was in Very Bad Taste. Yet the Guide Dogs Association, a body perhaps more committed to the welfare of the blind than those letter-writers, was delighted with the cartoon and asked if they could have the original so they could have it framed.

Tragic death or great heroism where they concern real people are also thought by some to be sacred areas barred to the cartoonist, though this can depend on how far away in time the relevant incident occurred. King Harold and his arrowed eye is okay, as are Marie Antoinette kneeling to Madame Guillotine and General Custer failing to stand at Little Big Horn (mind, these two are foreigners). But the death of Nelson and Gordon of Khartoum

'You know what JB said, Sir George – you've got to learn to delegate.'

Sexual performance, the blind, and the Captain Oates incident – areas of humour some people would claim to be in doubtful taste. Even so, to me all these cartoons are funny.

are not okay, and Captain Oates walking to his death in the snow is *certainly* not okay (but see McMurtry's strip, below). We English are very sensitive about our heroes. There is less worry over anonymous deaths in history – the sinking of the *Titanic,* the *Hindenburg* disaster, the St Valentine's Day Massacre, and the like, are all quite acceptable. But the massacre at Mai Lai is *not* so, except when the cartoon is making some satirical comment on that incident.

Black, or sick, humour is a genre that has not attracted the cartoonist very much – not in this country, anyway. If you come across jokey decapitations, hangings, deformities, and blood-lettings in their most explicit form they are more likely to have been drawn by a Frenchman or a Japanese; on this side of the water, alas, our cartoonists seem not yet ready for these upper reaches of sophistication. English black humour tends to be expressed in throw-away wisecracks or dead-pan anecdotes or stylish film scripts (for example, *Kind Hearts and Coronets*); in

*'No, Bill, leave him. It's his decision. One of us had to
go to give the others a chance . . .'*

'Harry, come back! . . . They brought a friend!'

'Frankly, if I'd known this lot would be here I don't think I'd have bothered to come.'

'I only just made it before
my Dad's vasectomy.'

cartoon form there's a good chance that the 'black' part of the humour will turn out to be too overt and therefore low on style and maybe this is why our best cartoonists have kept away from it. One or two of them, however, have been able to control it, have in fact pushed the black element into the background and brought the clownish fantasy part well to the front. Ronald Searle achieved this with his St Trinian's schoolgirls and Charles Addams uses it as his stock in trade; in neither case is there anything remotely nasty about the results. Other cartoonists, other ends. There are some who aspire towards fine art and who use their drawing skill to shock and repel, which means that the humour content becomes wafer thin or sometimes disappears altogether. The cartoon has then ceased to be a cartoon but unwittingly presents itself as a dark aperture through which we can see the creator's state of mind. Apropos of that, it has been remarked that a close study of any cartoonist's work can reveal a lot about his psychological make-up and way of life and this is particularly true when we consider the products of the 'sick' brigade. Pop night-school psychology this may be, but any such assumptions we make can also be laid at the door of plain commonsense.

Satire

'Without humour, satire is invective; without literary form, it is
mere clownish jeering.' Thus said Richard Garnett. But what is
satire? It is another of those words, I'm afraid, which everybody is
clear about yet somehow unable to agree about – there's never any
certainty when someone uses it that it is going to have quite the
same meaning to anyone else. In the 1960s we heard a lot about
satire when *That Was the Week that Was* and similar TV shows
were bouncing their quips into our living-rooms, and though it was
commonly asserted that these were satirical shows, the more exact
were complaining that they were not satires at all but lampoons.

There is also a tendency to bring in Jonathan Swift whenever
satire is mentioned; even people who have never read Swift (and
reckon his *Gulliver's Travels* to be a story only for children) find the
opportunity to slot his name into conversation. On higher literary
levels Aristophanes and Juvenal and Pope might appear and if this
happens we can assume that the people engaged in the discussion
are using the word in a more precise and traditional way. To them
satire is not merely cock-snooking or a two-fingered gesture but is
a literary form that uses ridicule, sarcasm, irony, wit and humour
for the purpose of exposing vice or folly, its final aim being to secure
change. In some ways it is a very *moral* activity. To be merely
sarcastic, ironic, or sardonic is not the same thing, but any of these,
coupled with wit and humour, can be an instrument used in satire
for the purpose of attack and amendment.

So what about satirical cartoons? If we keep reasonably close to

'There was a vacancy, but
I'm afraid it's been filled.'

Compare this with the Langdon
strip on pages 40–41. I hope you
agree that it is a sweet
come-uppance.

55

In the early 'sixties I wrote and drew a weekly feature called *Types Behind the Print* – forty mildly astringent comments on the world of journalism and literature. After that I did occasional features, to a similar formula, among which were Motor Types, Admen, Medical People, Theatre Types, and The British Abroad. Here are a few examples taken at random.

(*Private Eye* has recently had a go at Great Bores, a series employing two writers and one cartoonist; Fleet Street was always over-manned.)

From: Advertising People

ADMAN PLUS Every Advertising Agency seems to have one of these types cluttering up the G-Plan fitments, generally in the Creative Department. Showy, ebullient, and shouldering a pink gin face latticed with hair, he is the kind of adman you expect to find only in a 'B' movie. On the surface he appears to be a jocular iconoclast but really he is a very crafty Yes-man, yet for all his apparent phoniness he has had one or two great ideas in his time. As he will remind you, given half a chance.

From: Television Types

There are telly reporters and telly reporters. The young ones crouch in their combat jackets and deal out chopped bits of sentences breathlessly to the camera; the old one (as here) finds a comfortable corner and extemporises a flow of world-weary chat to no one in particular, a calloused Fleet Streeter who has globe-trotted through twenty-five years of foreign correspondence, a disillusioned cynic who maintains he has seen it all before. His spiel is literate, down-beat and humane. The bar-room props (again, as here) never vary.

From: The British Abroad

'Quite the prettiest part of County Cork, don't you agree? We have a bit of rough shooting and, of course, excellent fishing – I hardly see Charles at all! Yes, we've been here two years now – we simply had to clear out. Can I say it? That horrid little man Wilson with his taxes and the Welfare State and that equality business – I tell you, life just wasn't worth living over there. Here's so different – the Irish are charming people, aren't they? We have a couple of the village gels living in and Mrs Breen does the cooking for me. No, I don't miss London at all – of course, Charles has to go over half a dozen times a year for his board meetings and I pop over occasionally to Harrods on a shopping spree. And remember that the *Telegraph* arrives by midday!'

From: Motor People

REV. COUNTER MAN His love affair with the Automobile remains as star-fixed now as it always was, though each of his sleek-lined mistresses seldom lasts longer than a year or two before being discarded for a new, more exciting beauty. He handles them skilfully and provocatively, but always safely. His requiem for each departed lover is always 'We just ran out of road'. However, he's beginning to wonder if he's not nearing the time when this kind of dalliance is slightly absurd for a man of his age.

continued ▶

Anticipation

Lucky me – he's promised me a private audition at his town flat afterwards

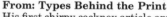

From: Theatre Types

THE ENTREPRENEUR AND THE MODEL His business interests are wide but they interlock very neatly. They include TV, theatres, stage shows, night clubs, boxing promotion, and actors' agencies. He is therefore a powerful figure in the world of showbiz, and actors must tread warily within his territory. A soft side to his character is shown by his willingness to help young people in their efforts to get on to the Stage. Here he is with his latest protégé at the First Night of a big American musical. 'This child has *talent*,' he says, 'and I expect great things from her.'

From: Types Behind the Print

His first chirpy cockney article appeared in The Friday Book and was all about his jellied-eel stall. Subsequently he wrote anecdotes (in chirpy cockney) about his news-stand in Leicester Square, his rag-and-bone business in Bermondsey, and the personalities who patronised his boot-black pitch in Piccadilly. Twelve months in jail provided the roughage for his first book, after which he was hugged to the bosom of Theatre Toolbench. Here he wrote the chirpy cockney lyrics for 'Cockney Sparrers Ain't 'Arf Chirpy'. In keen demand for the smarter Chelsea parties, he always gives his hosts their money's worth with his unbroken flow of cuss-words and invented prison slang. A non-drinker, he turns in a reliable boozy act for TV.

From: Advertising People

COPY-WRITER Three years among the dreaming spires, chiselling away through layers of Beowulf and the Development of the Novel towards a final Honours Degree, and here he is now at the KW and D Agency, paring down a slogan for instant coffee. 'Render, render down to the essential oils,' he has said, 'and ka-pow! you've got it. "Beanz Meanz Heinz." Beautiful, that, beautiful. Joycean, with a touch of Ogden Nash, would you say? No, I'm happy – I'm content – I don't go home each night to work on the obligatory TV play about a conscience-stricken adman. Just give me a Colour Supplement to browse through.'

You are never alone with a ... POW

that more traditional definition, then a great number of what we normally call political cartoons must be satirical both in method and intent. Then there are inevitably the blurred edges where, say, a social comment cartoon leans over into the satire category, and, of course, there is mild satire as well as sharp satire. Occasionally a cartoonist appears on the scene who is not only equipped with the necessary wit and drawing ability but is also a person whose disposition towards the world is a critical one, a person who regards the capers of his fellow humans with somewhat meagre benevolence but a great deal of cynicism. When this happens the cartoons he may produce can be very powerful indeed. Nevertheless he is a rarity; what is more usual is the cartoonist who can turn it on and off, or more precisely, one who can be provoked by only a limited number of targets. Certain things irritate him and it's for these that the bottle of acid is brought out. The trouble is, of course, that once somebody gets a reputation as a sword-wielding iconoclast and terror of the mighty (and this applies to professional satirists of all kinds) he is expected to play that part all the time, and if he adopts that role much of what he does is bound to be spurious. He has to scratch around for targets which in the process become inevitably more and more trite and unworthy. But as I said, this chap is something of a rarity – most of the others find it very easy to move in and out, perhaps doing zany or social comment cartoons one day and shooting off a satirical barb the next. Also very rare is real vindictiveness; what we get most of all is a rather mild astringency or subdued scorn – which can be quite effective because if we in this country respond to anything at all we respond to understatement.

'My people! The hated dictatorship is over! From now on, you will elect me democratically!'

Topical

I understand that journalists hold the TV review column to be the best sinecure of them all; money, as they say, for old skipping rope. The topical 'pocket' cartoon, perhaps unfairly, is looked at in a similar light by many cartoonists– a cushy number, they are apt to say, with plenty of loot attached. Usually on the front page of newspapers, sometimes in topical weeklies, it is a comfortable little slot to occupy. It is there on its own, surrounded by hard news and no competition within sight. The cartoonist is usually under contract and his job is to fill that hole four or five times a week. The essence is topicality– that comes first; the quality of the idea comes second. In a way it is similar to a stand-up comedian ad-libbing at some late-comers clattering about in the stalls. He is seen to be thinking on his feet, quick stuff to the moment – and the audience loves it merely because it *is* quick and spontaneous. This is partly the attraction of the topical pocket cartoonist – the idea is down

Patrick Catling once wrote of Handelsman: 'He has the quietly sardonic appearance and manner of a middle-aged American intellectual close to the end of a self-imposed endurance test.' Once you have that picture in your mind then you realise that his cartoons could be no other than what they are.

'Quite right, too! I myself
have always made a point of
cutting Mr Wilde.'

An Osbert Lancaster
pocket-cartoon from the *Daily
Express,* and one from Marc, of
The Times.

there, next to the news item it is joking about and the reader
marvels that it's been done so quickly. That doesn't mean that all
pocket cartoons are hawking run-of-the-mill ideas – that head boy
of all pocket cartoonists, Osbert Lancaster, has long since been
picked out as an exception that proves the rule. He is essentially
stylish, and there is no argument that his upper-middle-class
world of Maudie Littlehampton is a very stylish creation, the ideas
he imposes on it having an urbanity and wit not too abundant in
daily journalism. Marc has contributed ideas of a similar quality to
the Diary column of *The Times*; both these men walk some distance away from the general run of horny-handed comic artists of
Grub Street. The field of operation of these two is the modes and
manners of a certain strata of society and through it they make
their acerbic comments on the passing scene. They are not gag men
as such. As for the quality of their drawing, Osbert Lancaster's is
professionally workmanlike if a little wooden; Marc, on the other
hand, retains the best qualities of the untrained amateur drawing
at the peak of his ability — in fact, this lack of facility gives him a
certain quirky advantage. That, coupled with a sharp sense of
observation, can sometimes make a Marc caricature particularly
devastating.

There are bigger set-piece topical drawings, of course, on the
inside pages of some papers – again, these contract cartoonists
work to tight deadlines, combing through the news for something
they can turn to their advantage, and it goes without saying that
there is never any shortage of raw material. Occasionally their
best ideas (and remember they are expected to submit several
'roughs' to their editor) can turn on some bizarre if minor news
item, a news item so minor there's a strong possibility that most
readers will have missed it. To get round this problem the cartoonist relies on that old stand-by, the newspaper within a newspaper – in other words, a drawn headline on a drawn newspaper.
And why not? It's a simple reminder.

Naturally enough, immediacy is less important in weekly papers and magazines because of the very fact that they *are* weekly.
Here the topicality of the cartoon has to be finely judged and a
certain amount of crystal-gazing has to be done in order to decide
whether the event recognised by the cartoon will still be in the
reader's mind on publication day. This means that the themes
treated in the weeklies are generally more weighty and important
and certainly less frivolous than those treated by the dailies.

Having stewed over the current newspapers all morning and
with the radio tuned to the news programme, the topical cartoonist
squeezes out his ideas and puts them down in the form of pencil
roughs. He has now to get one of them accepted by the editor and
here he enters a world that can have more than a few touches of
surrealism about it.

Many newspaper editors are not unlike generals; they set the
viewpoint, the strategy, the tone of their newspaper, delegating
particular areas of operation to their brigadiers and colonels and
avoiding all connection with the job of putting the nuts and bolts
together. Only when the tasks are completed and the finished
edition is lying there hot from the press do they scrutinise it in any
detail; it is then that they make their comments and criticisms and

'What's in it for me?'

'MAC' of the *Daily Mail* is Stanley McMurtry. This drawing appeared at the time of the Lockheed bribery scandals.

When a news item revealed that certain troops operating in plain clothes in Northern Ireland had been carrying bogus Press cards for use in an emergency, Raymond Jackson (JAK) made this comment about it in the London *Evening Standard*. It is a typical JAK drawing – strong, very butch, well organised, precise in detail. (But not precise in *every* detail: see pages 84-5.)

nes, The Mirror – Smith, The Sun – Miller, Express – and it's The Gay News again for you, Huck!'

'All this TV violence is ruining my carpet!'

The cartoons I have so far chosen for inclusion in this book have been pitched at a certain level — they have been what might be called 'up-market' cartoons. And if there is up-market, then there must necessarily be down-market. The more robust, knock-about, uncomplicated end of the trade is a large one, scattered throughout the popular press and often occupying boxed-in features with titles like 'LAFF THIS OFF'. The drawings themselves have a certain sameness, crude but workmanlike, and the artists tend to have pen-names like Butch or Wacko or Mick.

In giving you the group on these two pages, I have to admit that I am cheating, for all these cartoons are spoofs created by four up-market cartoonists for a *Punch* parody of a TV magazine. Good parody always crystallises the style and character of the original, and I believe these drawings do just that.

LEW EDGAR

'Not a very good pitcher!'

FRED.

'I'll be glad when this series is over — it must be costing a fortune hiring that lot every week!'

SMACK.

'Funny, it usually works when my dad kicks it.'

approvals. Of course, this is a matter of degree: it is claimed that one knighted editor read every word in his paper before it was committed to the press, and then there was the other one who spent most of his time travelling in foreign climes apparently quite content to let his staff get on with it. But there is one tiny little bolt most of these editors will not delegate, and that is the choosing of the topical cartoon. This decision is one they seem to revel in, even though the cartoonist (a wily bird, usually aided and abetted by the features editor) has his ways and means of manipulating the choice towards the cartoon idea *he* wants to draw. At one national newspaper recently the editor was so ignorant of the grammar and syntax of cartooning (he was barely able to 'read' a drawing) that the natural thing for him to do would be to acknowledge this blind spot in his make-up and give this little job over to someone else. But no, he persisted each day in going through a bizarre pantomime with the cartoon roughs until he had been guided and prodded and persuaded into making his own decision. His next remark would then reveal that he had missed the point of the drawing altogether; once outside in the corridor the cartoonist and features editor were known to fall about quite helplessly. But the ritual had been observed and everyone was happy.

'On behalf of my husband – yes, we're definitely in favour of twenty-four hour TV!'

Having said all that it might not be too perverse to admit that these editors could possibly be right in keeping direct control of these humorous drawings. The value of the cartoons to the newspaper can be out of all proportion to the space they occupy; not everybody reads the first leader but everybody looks at the cartoon, and if the paper has been fortunate in securing a cartoonist whose qualities and characteristics are unique and on the right wavelength for that paper, then the editor has on his books a very valuable property indeed. This kind of cartoonist can mean more to the circulation figures than any other single item and can quite often bind a reader's loyalty when everything else is telling him to cut adrift.

Some of these cartoonists are able, too, to work a nice line in 'spin-offs'. They manage this by introducing all kinds of extraneous goods into their drawings and more often than not these goods are booze. So boxes of whisky and cases of champagne are pushed into various corners of the drawing, their brand names carefully legible. And if it is necessary to show some technical object such as a duplicating machine or a combine harvester, those objects won't be extemporised in any haphazard way but will be particular models drawn very accurately. When the drawing is published it's reasonably certain that this bait will be taken and that champagne company or that whisky company will be quick on the telephone with an offer for the original artwork – and the offer will be a payment in kind. The duplicating machine and combine harvester people will tend to offer money. I know one cartoonist who quite innocently and purely as a touch of local colour once included a construction worker with the firm's name across the back of his donkey jacket; that firm bought the original. It also bought the next drawing in which there was a similar construction worker. It

'It's another repeat!'

63

Carl Giles, perhaps the most popular of all British cartoonists and a great asset to the *Daily Express:* this example is recognition humour with a vengeance, backed up with a mass of extraneous happenings and telling detail. (It is this sub-text that can be properly labelled 'Gilesean'.)

will not surprise you that from then onwards that construction worker kept appearing regularly.

Perhaps the prime example of a cartoonist who has a loyal, loving 'readership' is Carl Giles of the *Daily Express,* an artist who has created in his drawings a warm-hearted Gilesean world which has tremendous reader-appeal. The doings of his 'family' throughout all these years have carved out an unassailable position for him at the popular end of the craft; he has had plenty of imitators but none has got anywhere near him in this respect. His basic ideas are not sophisticated or particularly witty, but they invariably strike the correct note and are true to the section of society he draws. And another point of attraction is the way he sprinkles his

'"George", I said, "Christmas Eve. What better time to ask our new neighbours round for a drink and meet Mummy".'

drawings with little touches of 'business', little sub-plots going on behind the sofa or outside the window or down the corridor – these are the extras that tighten his hold on his readers as much as the fact that he draws correctly in the 'naturalistic' manner with no violent distortions. (Even his swarm of little lads is acceptable enough.) His settings are very *real*; for instance, no one has drawn the old urban elementary school with such insight and accuracy. And he seldom raises his voice; any criticisms implied in his cartoons are quiet, parochial affairs closely in line with the attitudes you associate with the readers of the *Daily Express*. Thus, for example, he is on the side of the motorist and the farming community and the old ways, and conversely he has that dyed-in-the-wool suspicion of foreigners and trendies and intellectuals. Yet his 'family' is solidly working-class and you can feel that his sympathies and affection lie there rather than with the petit-bourgeois strata the *Express* aims at. He is a hot property, all right, and it is probable that he has a better and more lucrative contract than any other cartoonist in Fleet Street.

Those are my main categories of cartoon humour: Recognition, Social Comment, Zany, Visual Puns, Black Humour, Satire, and Topical. There are, additionally, one or two sub-divisions – those oddities which are here today and quite possibly gone tomorrow, those minor branch lines that carry little traffic and frequently finish at a dead-end.

A nice observation, this, on the use of colloquial idiom. There is no delayed flick to the cartoon but a steady build-up of effect. And look at Scully's drawing style – marvellously free and autographic but with a tight control over the use of tone. You are always aware of *space* in a Scully drawing.

'Oh stop worrying about her – he's not serious. All he ever talks about is Vietnam,
Rhodesia, the balance of payments crisis, China and the Bomb.'

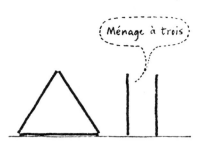

Geometric

To compete in an egg and spoon race there are two basic requirements – you must have an egg and you must have a spoon. If you
line up at the start holding a spoon minus the egg (or even an egg
minus the spoon) it is likely that you will be disqualified right
away. Similarly, if you wish to compete as a cartoonist there are
also two basic requirements: you must be able to think up ideas
and you must be able to draw them. Or so one would imagine. Yet
there are people who have been able to find a way round these
qualifications and these are people who have plenty of ideas but
who are hopeless at drawing. What they do is use the Geometric-
Symbol method, a method tailor-made for those non-artists who
have pretensions towards sophistication. They reduce the whole
visual world to the simple geometric shapes that can be accomplished with the aid of a pen and ruler (and for the more advanced,
compasses, too). Lines are made to fall in love with Dots; Squares
play tricks on Rectangles; Flamboyant Polygons lord it over Simple Triangles. It is all so very, very cute. And if the captions can be
got into French, so much the better (after all, this type of cartoon
appears only in the egg-head weeklies). By way of example I have
knocked out a couple of pastiche ideas myself (I'm as dab a hand
with the pen and ruler as the next man).

Faux-naif

When an ideas man *can* draw but cannot develop a satisfactory
comic style of *cartoon* drawing, he quite often throws in the towel
and adopts a deliberately childlike style. (Other accomplished
draughtsmen attempt cartooning by going for a violently grotesque style at first, then once that is out of their system they settle
down to something less self-conscious.) And there's no doubt about
it, this childlike, naïve style can be very arresting, its effects being
gained by a simple, pseudo-sophisticated directness. Cluttered
they are not. Barry Fantoni, an accomplished painter of neo-realist
portraits and a fine draughtsman, opts for the Faux-naif style in
his cartooning and because he *can* draw well he has to push his
cartoon method to the opposite extreme. Another exponent of the
faux-naif approach is Mel Calman (but so often does he protest his
inability to draw perhaps we should make that true-naif). His
rudimentary little people have a cosy charm and the way they are
rendered has about it an aura of fashionable smartness, though I
believe his little quips could exist quite happily without any drawings being attached to them at all. But then they wouldn't be
cartoons.

Barry Fantoni can draw in the
realist/naturalist manner but he
elects to do his cartooning in a
kindergarten style – a very
effective one in his hands.

'Honestly, officer, ask Miss
Warburton, I did it all myself'.

When you see this sort of picture of England in Springtime, you have to look carefully through the piece of fine prose underneath before you realise it is an advertisement for United Investment Trusts, Ltd., or somebody's beer. But there is less difficulty . . .

This is what might be called a Two-Stage Reversal joke – a what-you-expect-and-what-you-get joke. It demonstrates Leslie Illingworth's faultless pen-and-ink technique, a technique which is essentially naturalistic yet masterly in its variety of textures, arrangement of tones, and subtle

. . . when you step out of doors and see England in Springtime itself.

atmospheric perspective. It is hardly cartooning, but this idea needs this kind of 'good' drawing. Note the quotes on 'good'. André François' scribbly, apparently childlike drawings elsewhere in the book are equally as 'good' because he, like Illingworth, fully realises his intention.

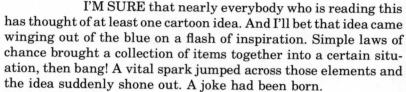

'Sorry, Not Quite'

I'M SURE that nearly everybody who is reading this has thought of at least one cartoon idea. And I'll bet that idea came winging out of the blue on a flash of inspiration. Simple laws of chance brought a collection of items together into a certain situation, then bang! A vital spark jumped across those elements and the idea suddenly shone out. A joke had been born.

As an art editor and one who has looked at many thousands of cartoons submitted by amateurs as well as professionals, I'd say it's an even bet that the idea you thought up was the one showing a police Black Maria with 'RUNNING IN – PLEASE PASS' on the back of it. There's been a tailing off recently but at one time I could be sure of seeing that joke at least once a month. And when you consider it, there is no difficulty in seeing how that idea came into being. The joke is one of those simple 'link' ideas bringing two separate areas together through a play on words. It comes about like this: You are walking down the street and you see a new car with a 'Running In' notice in the back window. That song with the chorus of coppers singing, 'We'll run them in, we'll run them in' leaps into your mind – and the next instant you have this image of a Black Maria hurtling away with that 'Running In' sign painted on the rear doors. You have thought up a joke; all that remains is to render it in a drawing.

I was fifteen when I thought of my first idea (*not* the Black Maria one). I recollect it featured a balletic navvy performing to an audience of hole-in-the-road watchers and it came back from *Punch* with a rejection slip and a pencilled note from Fougasse, the art editor at that time. That was my 'one-off' idea and my career as a cartoonist came to a stop there. Or rather, it was shelved. Nine years later I was in the office of *Lilliput* with a large portfolio of serious illustration specimens; I had just come out of art school and was doing the rounds of the magazines. James Boswell, the art

editor of *Lilliput*, went through my wonderful specimens with the speed of a hustler dealing a pack of cards. They were not, he pondered . . . , they were not the right *flavour* for *Lilliput* (that word 'flavour' is the nicest of possible let downs; it covers a multitude of interpretations). Then he idly flicked through a sketch book I had brought along. 'Why not draw that larger and send it in,' he said. 'I won't promise anything but it's worth a try.' 'That' was a cartoon idea. It featured Stonehenge and made droll play with the Domino Theory. I sent it in and it was accepted and I was paid eight guineas. I decided to become a cartoonist.

Atchison, an Australian, has produced here a rather mechanical idea – you can see the thought processes very plainly. But it is a perfectly valid piece of cartoon construction.

It is now that I must stress the major quality essential to any successful cartoonist. Persistence. Persistence to keep sending in drawings week after week for months on end without making a sale. Gradually, through practice, the ideas get better and the drawing style develops. Eventually there is a first acceptance, then after that the distance to the second is shorter, and so on until these intervals diminish and the frequency of success becomes more certain. But not absolutely. The professional cartoonist's life is a hazardous one in that respect; everything he does is speculative and he knows that even when he is firmly established his rejections will outnumber his acceptances somewhere in the ratio of four to one. Uncertainty always has him by the elbow.

Of course, there are a few characters who blaze with success right from the word go, but these are rather rare. To most, a commitment to cartooning as a solo occupation needs the kind of temperament that lies close to foolishness. Only when someone is established well enough and has hammered out a distinctive style do the commissions come along to make his income reasonably definite – possibly a contract with a newspaper, a regular spot in a magazine, humorous illustration and decoration, or drawing for advertising. Again, this is not the predominant pattern; a fair

BETTER WATCH THIS, FRIGTHORNE— WE'RE PRODUCT-TESTING THE NEW IMPROVED FOAMO

OO! A SHINING SHEIK!

AT YOUR SERVICE, LOVELY LADY

Zany with satirical overtones. Detergents and all the hard-sell that goes with them is a regular target for cartoonists.

number of the best cartoonists around these days are people who keep a lifeline to another occupation. Yet it seems that some readers have the idea that a magazine like *Punch* employs a whole roomful of staff humorists who sit beavering away at their drawing boards in order to produce each week's quota of gags. In fact, the thirty or so people who draw regularly for *Punch* are scattered right across England with just their friendly neighbourhood GPO to act as go-between. (There's a particularly strong contingent in the Manchester/Liverpool area, incidentally.)

How then, do these people get their ideas? Everyone seems to have his own very idiosyncratic method. Those fully-fashioned ideas plucked out of the air are (unfortunately for the cartoonist) very rare birds indeed; more usual are the grinding 'ideas sessions' where the cartoonist takes himself off to some quiet corner and slowly sweats them out. 'The hardest part of my job,' James Thurber once said, 'is to convince my wife that I am working when I am standing staring out of the window.' David Langdon came

Fashion (women's trouser suits, unisex, turtle-neck jerseys, long hair) banging against the carapace of the rule book. An unusual area for Breeze; his happy stamping ground is Royalty on the blink and fly-blown Beckettian tramps.

'Rules are rules. Either she's wearing trousers, or he's not wearing a tie.'

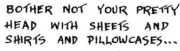

nearest to defining this process when he called it 'controlled mind wandering'. The process goes something like this: a subject is selected, then the mind is allowed to wander on a loose lead into, around and through that subject. Because the cartoonist has that kind of mind certain links and jumps will occur, certain apparently illogical connections will be made, and thus the basis of an idea will be roughly cast. It's at this point that the craftsman comes in to refine it, take it one step further, hone and polish it. Having got this far there is a quick surge of adrenalin at the achievement; the cartoonist knows he's got something and all he has to do now is express it in terms of drawing. But he also knows that somewhere a cartoon editor or art editor or even an editor has yet to assess it for publication. If he is working regularly for one magazine he knows the level it aims at and tries to match his ideas to that, but even then he can never be sure how they will be received; cartoonists are notorious for believing their best ideas are rejected while their make-weights get through. I think this is perfectly understandable because if humour is absolutely subjective as I've been suggesting all along, then the chap who does the choosing is no less subjective than anyone else. In most publications the sieve that accepts or rejects these offerings is just another human being, one

73

'. . . And then came the war.'

Albert Rusling and Ionicus (Jos Armitage) are both part of that strong contingent of cartoonists living in the northwest of England; this Albert drawing is a nice delayed sight-gag, while Ionicus gives us a quiet comment on human frailty.

who is exposed to all those little pressures on his judgment such as the state of his liver or whether he has lunched too long and too well or whether he has just had a row. This being so, he might accept tomorrow what he rejects today. And vice versa.

The ideal cartoon editor would be above such hazards, of course. He would also be completely open-minded about all shades of humour and he would appreciate the whole spectrum of humour. He would be encyclopaedic in his general knowledge, particularly on world events, local events, history, literature, art, music, politics, films, television, social changes, customs, sport, all human activities – in fact, just about everything. Above all, he would be completely steeped in his own national popular culture, because it is from this deep pool that so many humorous ideas are netted. However, those who do the choosing are not always up to these measures. There are discrepancies. There are gaps. Who knows, there might be umpteen sublimely witty cartoons lying dog-eared and unpublished because the editors who considered them were just plain ignorant.

There is an auxiliary question. Should the person choosing cartoons be a cartoonist himself? Not necessarily, but having that experience can hardly go amiss. He stands between the creator and the reader, testing for brightness – and if the idea is good but the drawing poorly organised as a vehicle for that idea, then he must be able to suggest how to put it right. The cartoonist himself, naturally enough, can never see his own work as the reader sees it – it is too familiar, the idea has been cajoled into existence, it has been developed through several phases. The reader, on the other hand, turns the page and click! the cartoon blinks its message.

So there, then, is a process through which this message, i.e. the

'Every week I tell him we don't sell the Church
Times or the Methodist Recorder . . .'

joke, is brought into being, except that I have not yet mentioned an essential yet indefinable ingredient. Joke-making cannot be learnt; at the end of the day it relies on a certain personality and character flux, a certain 'bent' that can summon sparks from nothing. Humorists are humorists only because they possess this particular flair. Cartooning, at its best, requires a peculiar and rare talent. Like juggling, it *looks* easy, but unlike juggling each session demands a brand new routine.

Names in the Household

Stop any person in the street and ask him to name a cartoonist and I think it most likely that they would offer one of these: Thelwell, Ronald Searle, Hargreaves, Russell Brockbank, Giles, or Bill Tidy. Possibly Osbert Lancaster and Gerald Scarfe. Even David Langdon might sneak in under the rope. Why those? Why not Mahood, ffolkes, Starke, Handelsman, Hector Breeze, or Heath? Well, each one in that first group has a label attached and in the second each has not. We like labels, categories, familiarities – so we know about Thelwell because he's the 'Pony Man', Searle has St Trinian's, Hargreaves his bird, Brockbank his motor cars. Giles has the Giles Family and Bill Tidy, well Bill Tidy as well as being a funny cartoonist is also a funny performer and appears on TV. Perhaps not household names in the full sense but they've got their feet in at the door. Specialising, tending the single furrow, they have gradually dug their way into the public's consciousness. (Successful specialisation does not automatically bring fame; those fans of *Bristow* and *Andy Capp* do not always remember that Frank Dickens and Smythe are their creators.)

Yet the greater part of Thelwell's output and certainly the better

I'm sure Tony Holland was inspired when he thought of this one; anything goes on tee-shirts these days, but this drawing has a cast-iron logic.

75

It is not only veteran-car buffs who can enjoy this Brockbank cartoon — we all warm to a demonstration of the classic old putting one over the garish modern. And that Rolls Royce Silver Ghost is no doubt accurate down to the last bolt head.

—Brockbank

'Ruddy sportsdays . . .'

quality part has nothing to do with ponies and little girls in jodhpurs. The Jennifers of the country's riding schools might be very surprised at the sharpness and astringency of his social comment cartoons. Similarly with Searle – the St Trinian's albatross still hangs heavily around his neck even though he stopped producing those cartoons umpteen years ago. The power of his satirical drawings and the excellence of his caricatures are properly recognised in certain quarters, of course, but the public at large clings resolutely to those hordes of rampaging schoolgirls. Brockbank, however, really loves the motor car and his cartoons get an answering chime from all those other devotees who admire his drawings because of their deadly accuracy of detail. Even so, Brockbank manages to make very adroit caricatures of every make of car he tackles. He is also able to suggest the movement of cars better than almost anyone else.

These are the cartoonists who can bask, if they like that sort of

Vintage St Trinian's, though Ronald Searle would prefer it if we forgot those rampaging schoolgirls.

thing, in a little patch of fame. What of the others? Well, all of us are Kilroys at heart, we all have that impulse to scratch our names on the wall to establish the fact that we are here, that we exist, no matter how much we deplore other graffiti when we see it. And cartoonists, like all makers of things throughout time, wish to claim their work as their very own by putting their signature on it. It is, after all, a small gesture of egotism, and thinking of those vast caverns on the North Circular Road where the British Museum stores one copy of each issue of every publication, it is also a tiny toe-hold on immortality.

LARRY established himself on the cartoon scene with his *Man in Apron* series of 'sight' jokes; later came *Man in Garden* and *Man in Office* but where I think he caught those rare flashes of truth was in the *Man in School* cartoons, coming as they did from his direct experience as a schoolteacher. His was not the *Magnet*, Harry Wharton world, but the glazed brick jungle of the Secondary Modern, and like Carl Giles he knew exactly where to touch that raw nerve of authenticity.

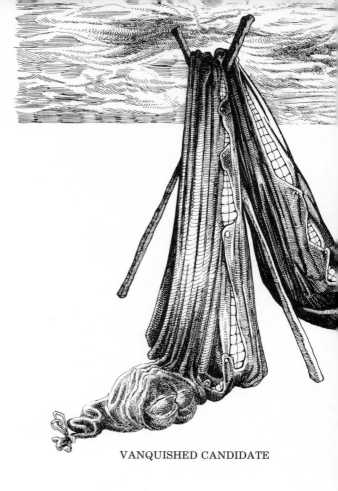

Grand Gothick from John Jensen. These examples have been extracted from a larger feature called 'Bodies Politic, USA' — a highly imaginative piece of visual metaphor. In addition to sheep and top-flight tennis players, Australia produces more cartoonists per acre than any other country. Jensen is one of them, and has been part of the London contingent for the last twenty-seven years.

VANQUISHED CANDIDATE

THE STATUS QUO CONTEMPLATES A POSSIBLE MOVE

PARTY DOGMATIST

THE CANDIDATE
HEDGES HIS BET

THE SILENT MAJORITY IN CHORUS

'May we use your phone?'

Unfunny – A Confession

SOME readers might now be wondering how I have managed to get this far without mentioning the Banana Skin. It seems that whenever two or three people are gathered together and discussing the subject of humour it isn't very long before one of them brings on the banana skin, for when other ideas are tenuous or tentative that piece of yellow peel provides us with one of the immutable truths. The creed goes something like this: If a haughty fat man (why is he always 'fat'?) steps on a banana skin and falls to the pavement, it is funny. If a little old woman slips on the skin, it is not funny. The fat man, because he is flaunting a sense of superiority, becomes a ridiculous and therefore funny figure when he inadvertently up-ends himself. Whether he hurts himself doesn't come into it – the incident is apparently funny regardless. Pomposity has been pricked. So 'Banana Skin' gets those capital initials because it is part of a solemn pronouncement which brooks no contradiction.

I can see the reasoning behind this and can understand why it is emphasised but I must confess that I don't find it funny myself, whether it happens to a pompous (fat) man or a nice little old lady or to anyone else you care to mention. That doesn't mean to say that I don't favour the humour of attack, but it must be the kind where the razor edge of satire is deliberately used in order to cut someone or something down to size; this kind is formalised and wit

Bruce Petty's ideas are nearly always placed in the centre of some violent action; action as it is happening or just after it has stopped happening.

'Clay too dry, Miss Melkin – too dry.'

When Logie Baird invented television he provided cartoonists with the nearest thing to a perpetual meal ticket. This example is a double-barrelled shot at TV programmes and a certain televiewing life style.

KenPyne

'I don't think the bedroom scenes are very convincing!'

is part of its engineering. The 'banana skin' is too *accidental,* too haphazard, and to me its key point (the falling down) is too simple a denouement to merit the label 'humour'.

A similar example which is sometimes cited maintains that a man falling down stairs is not funny, unless he has just warned his wife to be careful on the stairs; the humour arises not from the calamity itself but from the behaviour that led up to it. Our reaction is not unlike the glee we undoubtedly feel at seeing someone fall into his own trap, and is fuelled by the functioning of that 'surprise' element I have stressed earlier. But again, could it not be something else, an element of cruelty, a delight in the misfortunes of others? It is hard to imagine that kind of personality kink as the general pattern, yet when you ruminate on this aspect of behaviour so many examples float to the surface that perhaps the strand of cruelty is more general than we would like to admit. Few people nowadays will laugh at the antics of a cat when someone has tied a tin can to its tail, but many more will find rich amusement at the sight of an elephant raised awkwardly on its hind legs and dressed in a ballet costume. All right, the elephant, being a simple animal, is not aware of the ridiculous spectacle it presents and maybe those people in the audience who find the sight distasteful are being over-sensitive, but it's a short step from that to laughing at the person who is walking around totally unaware of the I AM A FOOL notice someone has pinned to his back. He is an innocent butt, and when we laugh at that we are certainly playing upon the least attractive reaches of our own psyche.

Envy, too, can intrude into this equation – we tend to be gleeful when an Expert is shown up to be less than expert and perhaps the

reason for this is that we secretly resent his superiority and so enjoy seeing him discomforted, but on the whole our laughing at others is pretty indiscriminate. (It is certainly true that some children and some primitive tribes derive much amusement from the mishaps that happen to others.)

So the Banana Skin Syndrome, then, is my blind spot. I also admit that when the banana skin is abstracted from the everyday world and put on to a stage or into a circus ring I can find it only marginally funny, and this I guess is a more serious failing. The fat man is here a performer, a clown, going through a set routine. The audience is aware of the routine and their expectancy is therefore primed. Does their laughter arise from relief that it is not they but the performers who are putting up with all that discomfort? Or has the audience been conditioned to believe that the main elements of slapstick, that is, simulated violence and real discomfort, are universally funny? The appreciation of slapstick must be either linked with our own basic aggressive feelings or something we learn; I tend to believe, as I have suggested is true of all humour, that slapstick is learned. This notion was first prompted by a documentary film I saw some years ago in which a little girl was shown watching a covey of clowns going through their act. She was about three years old and she was at the circus for the first time. It was plain that the violence going on in the ring was causing her some distress. At the same time she was aware that all the older kids around her were laughing fit to burst – so her face showed distress at the violence alternating with bafflement at the laughter. Being

These drawings (the first by JAK, the second by Bill Tidy, and the third by Walt Disney) are bound together by a common oddity. JAK and Tidy are not obviously dissimilar in character, but how does Mickey Mouse get into the same company? The solution to the puzzle lies in their hands. The drawn hands. JAK, Tidy and Disney invariably restrict the digits to three fingers and one thumb. Now why do they do this? My guess is that Disney humanised his animals' paws in the simplest way, possibly as an aid towards better animation, and this has had a subliminal influence on JAK and Tidy. Neither of these cartoonists could give me a satisfactory explanation beyond the notion that the correct number of fingers 'would seem overcrowded'.

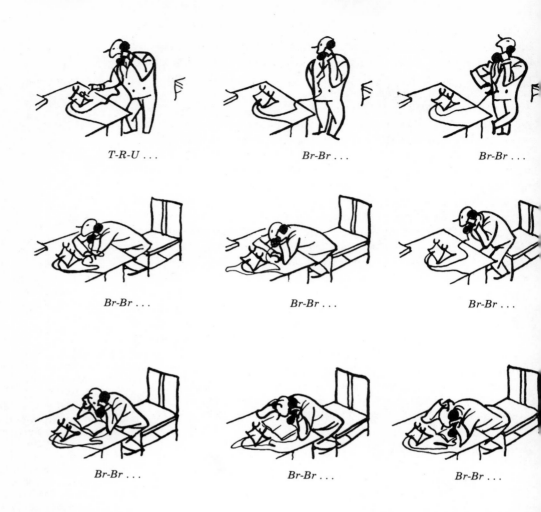

T-R-U . . .   *Br-Br . . .*   *Br-Br . . .*

Br-Br . . .   *Br-Br . . .*   *Br-Br . . .*

Br-Br . . .   *Br-Br . . .*   *Br-Br . . .*

a bright girl it took only a few more seconds for her to learn that what the clowns were doing was meant to be laughable – after all, wasn't everyone around her laughing?

Cartoon Slapstick

Can you clown in cartoons? Is it possible to draw slapstick? Clowning is purely visual and cartoons are mainly visual, but one major element divides them – physical action. Cartoons are very static and fixed in time no matter how skilful they are in explaining what has gone before and what might happen in the future, or in giving us the semblance of actual movement. Only when they are reprocessed into the form of an animated cartoon film do they measure up to real clowning – not only measure up but go beyond. In a *Tom and Jerry* cartoon we are distanced from reality by the style of drawing and the fact that it is a drawn cat and a drawn mouse who are acting the roles of the clowns. (The bizarre and comical costume of actual clowns work only partially – we are still aware of the real people inside.) Now this 'distancing' enables me to accept the extreme and fantastic violence of Tom and Jerry as genuine humour. Tom does not merely fall down elegantly or blink through custard on his face, he is clobbered in all manner of ways, some so

This strip sequence has not been over-stretched; it needs something in the order of twenty 'frames' to express the passage of time and the contortions of the protagonist. Kenneth Bird was a master of this particular genre – note how his simple technique catches unerringly the way people behave at the telephone. T-R-U, incidently, was the code before Subscriber Trunk Dialling was introduced, and required the services of the Operator. Kenneth Bird took his pen-name – Fougasse – from the French word for a small anti-personnel mine used in the '14 –'18 War. Cartoons, he felt, relied on a similar 'squib' explosive effect.

86

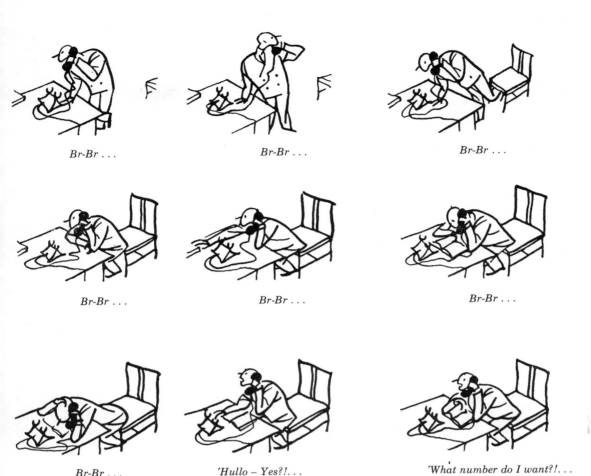

Br-Br . . .   Br-Br . . .   Br-Br . . .

Br-Br . . .   Br-Br . . .   Br-Br . . .

Br-Br . . .   'Hullo – Yes?!. . .   'What number do I want?!. . .

surreal the 'violence' no longer matches up to what we normally mean by that word. What keeps us watching and gives us amusement is the sheer anarchic fantasy and inventiveness of it all.

The only way a magazine cartoon can begin to approach this form is through the 'strip' technique, in which the artist provides us with the static 'master frames' from a non-existing animated sequence. These master frames are the key points in the story, the minimum number of pieces of information that we need to give us the sequence of the story, and through them we get a rudimentary display of action and movement and an extension of time. And like single-drawing cartoons the point of enlightenment is usually delayed to the final 'pay-off' frame.

In earlier days the French cartoonist Caran d'Ache and our own H.M. Bateman used this formula to great effect but their strips were generally flawed by being stretched out sometimes to the borders of boredom – too many frames giving unnecessary information. (One Bateman sequence used fifty-eight frames to show a musician leaving his home to play one note on his clarinet in a concert and then return home again.) Nearer our own time Giovanetti and now Hargreaves have proved that a whole plot needs no more than six or seven pictures. Hargreaves owes this, I

'I say, I'm most frightfully sorry' . . .

'I'm terribly afraid I've forgotten.'

A two-picture strip by Quentin Blake which he did to decorate an article on art school reminiscences.

think, to his early training with the Rank Organisation's cartoon film studio at Cookham – a studio headed by an ex-Disney man, which explains the Disney-like expertise of Hargreaves' animal drawing and animation. It is worth studying a strip by this cartoonist in some detail. Take, for instance, one of his 'Sparrow' strips – you will see that the bird is accurate in all essentials, that its movement is skilfully rendered with just the right amount of caricature, that its 'face' is able to take on all the variations of expression possible to the human face. The humour here is rooted in *human* behaviour; this bird, although it is correctly confined within its own bird world, is funny because its activities are based on one particular human foible or another and it is recognition of these foibles that provides the humour.

Many other cartoonists use the strip from time to time; Fougasse employed it particularly effectively in his bitter-sweet comments on the modes and manners of the middle class, while Handelsman, Heath and McLachlan all find its form a useful propellant for their satirical barbs.

Artistic Development: Stage One

Artistic Development: Stage Two

A sequence from Harry Hargreaves' highly regarded 'Sparrow' strip.

The Strip Cartoon

There is another variety of cartoon strip: reverse the order of those words and you define those daily offerings in the popular papers, the adventure and humorous serials which jerk their characters through endless escapades – the Strip Cartoon. Some of these humorous strips straddle both camps; the situation and central character are fixed and permanent but the humorous idea is self-contained and rounded off each day. The cartoon characters establish continuity and brand-appeal; the quick daily idea gives the customers immediate satisfaction.

The front runner in this field is probably the *Bristow* strip by Frank Dickens in the London *Evening Standard,* a strip brilliant in the simplicity of its conception. Bristow is the eponymous hero, a mild-mannered little clerk in the Buying Department of a firm whose enormous office is not unlike the Shell building on the South Bank; he is a subject of a state within a state and the main protagonist in the multifarious office goings-on. Frank Dickens is a humorist of impressive subtlety, someone who brings a very personal colouring to that category I have called Recognition Humour and it is upon this score that his popularity rests. His ideas are quiet but deep.

I'll mention only three other comic strips, not because I have regard for no others but because two of these creations lie deepest in my memory and the third is undoubtedly a curiosity.

Smokey Stover is something of a nostalgia trip for me; an American strip by Bill Holman, it was syndicated over here in the old

Two examples of the *Bristow* strip with its quiet and subtle humour. The 'twitch! twitch!' drawn in the second one is in the way of being a Frank Dickens trade mark, though it usually takes the form of couplets like 'ingratiate ingratiate', or 'smoulder smoulder'.

Two frames from Bill Holman's 'Smokey Stover' strip – a creation that owed more to its surreal detail and terrible incidental puns than to its storyline.

Everybody's Weekly and it chronicled the crazy world of one Smokey Stover, a fireman, and his running conflict with the fire-station superintendent. The plots were not very extraordinary but the manner in which they were set out certainly was, a kind of illogical surrealism nearer to Dali and The Goons than to Lewis Carroll and Edward Lear. Chairs were shaped like, in fact *were*, cupped hands, walking-sticks were tipped with castor wheels, and when the characters moved, nuts and bolts were seen to be dropping away from them. At moments of total exasperation the superintendent was drawn in an advanced state of disintegration: shirt buttons pinged, bow-tie flew, spectacles leapt from nose, his hair, mat-like, levitated one foot above his head and his teeth hopped into mid-air, snapping like a set of castanets. But there were other layers: in the background to each frame all kinds of quite extraneous Happenings were going on, involving pictures and objects and name-tags and an eccentric cat called Foo. This strip was really a major comic creation, packed with ideas, yet I have not seen it featured in any of those earnest anthologies serving up the Comic Strip as Popular Culture.

My second example is *Chelm of Tryg 2,* by our own Bill Tidy, a weekly two-line strip that ran for twelve months in *Punch* in 1966.

CHELM OF TRYG 2 by Bill Tidy

CHELM OF TRYG 2 by Bill Tidy

Again, the basic idea behind *Chelm* was an inspired one: Tryg 2 was a space station of the future, an orbiting Heathrow serving our planets and the galaxies beyond. Chelm was the major-domo, an ex-Army, District Commissioner type who ran the station with the kind of loose-reined paternalism we associate with the nine-teenth-century Raj. Within that framework Tidy exploited his own brand of zaniness to the full, making absolutely no concessions to those readers unable to tune to his wavelength but keeping his fantasy firmly planted in genuine human behaviour. We all know that unfettered fantasy, like dreams, is a dead bore because it means that nothing is impossible therefore nothing can surprise. This trap beckons anyone who sets his theme into a sci-fi future but Tidy steered clear of that hazard with no trouble at all.

The Upside-Downs of Little Lady Lovekins and Old Man Muffaroo was created in the early 1900s by Gustave Verbeek, an artist

There's no doubt that Bill Tidy's *Fosdyke Saga* and *Cloggies* strips have a large and faithful following, but my personal favourite has always been *Chelm*. Tryg 2 was an inspired invention and I live in hope that some day this British space station will become fully operational once again.

THE UPSIDE-DOWNS OF LITTLE LADY LOVEKINS AND OLD MAN MUFFAROO

1. In the canoe is an enormous fish that Lovekins and Muffaroo have caught.

2. Lovekins takes the fish on shore, while Muffaroo pushes off in the canoe to see if he can catch another.

3. Unluckily he hooks a sword-fish, and there is trouble right away. The old man fights bravely. The sword-fish dives;

4. Then he comes up again, and this time he thrusts his sharp snout right through the bottom of the canoe. Muffaroo tries to get the sinking boat to the nearest shore.

5. Just as he reaches a small grassy point of land, another fish attacks him, lashing furiously with his tail.

6. The canoe sinks in the sea which has now become choppy, but Muffaroo jumps ashore, safe and sound, and starts back across the point to rejoin Lovekins.

of no mean talent but mainly a man who pushed masochism into a completely new territory. Using a six-frame format for his stories he extended them to twelve frames by making each panel serve twice. After reading the sequence through the six pictures you then turned the strip upside down and read them again. So the mind-cracking task that Verbeek set himself was two-fold: firstly, each picture had to be composed so that it made sense either way one looked at it, and secondly, the story had to develop through twelve pictures (which were, let me remind you, contained in six panels). So ceiling and floor, sky and land, and all objects and animals, had to be interchangeable. His protagonists also had to be interchangeable – Lovekins when turned upside-down became Muffaroo, and vice versa. This required a high level of ingenuity but where Verbeek really stretched himself on the rack was when he made each panel carry two parts of the same story, the first frame being also the last and those in between developing the plot and drawing it to a conclusion *at the same time*.

This feature appeared in the New York *Herald* each week between 1903 and 1905, and though it is easy to think otherwise there is no evidence that it drove Verbeek into any madhouse.

How to do a twelve-frame strip in six pictures, by Gustave Verbeek. The mind boggles at the man's sheer ingenuity, but at the end of the day we wonder if it was all worth it.

Some cartoon ideas get by quite happily even though we might have some reservations about them; this one by Whittock is as complete as any cartoon could be.

'I don't know, but if it's a homing pterodactyl, it's a bit bloody late . . .'

95

'That's funny – it looks a perfectly normal,
ordinary, common-or-garden dog.'

Siggs' cartoons at their best are
extremely finely balanced; he
does not take us directly to the
target but sends us through a
series of ricochets until we reach
the bull's eye from an oblique
angle. His cartoons have the knack
(and the charm) of seeming at first
sight to be not nearly as good as
they are. After you get the point, a
Siggs cartoon is worth a few extra
moments of contemplation –
these can be quite rewarding.

'Pardon me, we're from New Orleans – would you call this foggy?'

'There's a car like ours.'

'Look, Mary, I must go; I started leaving
my husband an hour ago.'

'Could you manage to put it right without finding anything else.'

The Continental Drift

Рисунок С. СПАССКОГО

WHENEVER two or three cartoonists are gathered together and they have exhausted the topic of Money and how much of it they are earning they will occasionally touch on the Daffodil and Tank Syndrome. This is an area of the cartoonist's art that sends some of them into colourful flights of derision. 'East European cartoons,' they cry, 'that's all they are – a tank driving round a daffodil! All very significant, all very profound! But where's the joke? Where's the humour?'

And to some extent this is our rather simplistic notion of the character of East European cartoons: scratchy little drawings with the appearance of being deeply symbolic, Emperor's Clothes drawings that tend to win prizes in international exhibitions, drawings that proclaim too loudly that they are the received truth. And after the Russian Army's invasion of Czechoslovakia in 1968 it is true that we had a spate of such cartoons not only from Czech fugitives and exiles but also from outraged artists in West Germany and France. Suitable variations were around to take note of the Vietnam war and the American presence there but in Britain these themes were treated in a rather more massive manner by way of the full-blown political cartoon; bent wire drawings of tanks and flowers were not our scene, apparently. Recently this genre seems to have gone to ground where it lies, no doubt, awaiting the next major act of international violence.

These drawings appear to be submitted to papers and magazines

That one above is from the Russian humour magazine, *Krokodil*; this particular idea seems to crop up everywhere. To the right is a less solemn variation on the Tank and Daffodil syndrome – this time from Brazil.

NO SMOKING

speculatively just like any ordinary joke cartoon and are quite often published alongside joke cartoons; in Britain comments on major political and international events are fairly well restricted to the few artists who are labelled 'political cartoonists' and who each have a regular commitment to one paper.

When we open our sights rather wider we see that European cartoon humour (in fact, practically all foreign work) appears to be as funny and as varied as it is in Britain or anywhere else. Like pop music it reaches into a single, vast international stockpot for its subject matter and visual syntax. Perhaps the Germans and the French and the Japanese go in for sick humour rather more than the rest of us but everything else is there: the war between the sexes, the home life of the little man, teenagers, hippies, doctors, drunks, sexy girls, bureaucracy, money, motoring, technology, ecology, children, animals, and so on. And the manner in which these are treated can be through recognition humour, or it can be zany or off-beat, with visual puns and surreal flights of fancy.

Some of the clichés we have learnt to live with here brazenly appear in foreign papers, too, because cartoonists are always interested in what their peers are doing elsewhere and, because of this, they speak a fairly universal language. Ideas are 'adapted' rather than plagiarised. There are differences in drawing style, of course, but there are also many similarities. Much of the East European and Russian work is unashamedly 'comical', a bit red-

The parrot idea – a very funny one, I think – is by Wessum, who is a Dutchman. With the other birds, however, we are once again seeing A Very Serious Comment on the way people prefer to live. Yes, East European. Polish, in fact.

nosed, perhaps, for our taste, but to balance that they attempt few of those West European flights of pretentiousness that try to masquerade as Art. It seems that in countries like Switzerland, Austria and West Germany cartooning is viewed much more seriously than it is here (that might look like a contradiction in terms but it isn't); Europeans can be very reverent about the most trite excursion into cartoon graphics and then go on to elevate the practitioner to a level much higher than any cartoonist deserves. The reason for this might be the fact that the Continent is not exactly over-stocked with top-flight cartoonists so the few there are get the full treatment and find themselves hoisted on to pedestals. Would other countries publish so many expensive, beautifully produced books, each devoted to one cartoonist and each with acres of white space and one spidery drawing per page? The true environment for cartoons, they appear to be saying, is the art gallery; we on the other hand, though conscious of the eloquence of many of our cartoonists, feel that the music hall is their natural stamping ground. If any attempted to dress themselves up in that rarefied Continental manner it's pretty certain they'd soon get a raspberry blown their way.

The means by which cartoonists pin their ideas down are many and varied – a number 6 brush, a sharpened twig, a standard Gillot nib; from the broad autographic sweep to the carefully worked up miniature. Jenö Dallos, the Hungarian cartoonist, belongs to this last group, a mapping-pen man who crochets his drawings together with infinite care. He is very much in the mid-European 'symbolist' tradition and like many others is now well into Environment and Pollution.

Yet there is a curious twist to this. Those British humorous artists most derisive about the daffodil/tank brigade would be the first to acknowledge the stature of – and their debt to – a Continental cartoonist, a Roumanian Frenchman called André François. It is true that most of his work was published in this country (in *Lilliput* and *Punch*) and that his main cartoon-producing period was in the 1950s, but his was a strangely different kind of humour and a different kind of drawing. It was not *humorous* drawing as we know it, or *straight* drawing; it was somewhat weird, slightly uncouth, and in certain respects childlike. But it gave off a pronounced aesthetic appeal, that indefinable something that told us that this man François was not merely a humorist but an artist in the deepest meaning of the word. Everything he did generated its own excitement – this being particularly true of the work he did in colour. Other cartoonists and art students recognised this quality and many benefited enormously from his influence (there is a School of François as there is a School of Searle and a School of Steinberg) but a large section of the general public was left completely unimpressed – in fact, they were positively anti-François. Those readers who found little to like in his work or even felt

My favourite André François cartoon. It is a short-story encapsulated within a single drawing, the salient facts expertly marshalled: the twin beds, the jacket with its black armband, the fur coat as a bedside mat, the man luxuriously stretching, the seraphic smile. Then note the way the man has been drawn: the tilt of his head, the position of his hands and arms, the accurate way in which his pyjamas have been observed. Incomparable!

'Don't trouble. I've found it.'

Four more from François. The one below is perhaps not one of his best ideas, but the drawing style is typical of that which could be infuriating to some readers and engaging to others.

outraged by it were reacting as they did because they considered it crude and simple, something their 'little Jimmy, who is five, could do standing on his head'. And it must be said that stylistically François' colour work – his cover designs and full-pages for *Punch*, his posters and his set-designs – did have the simple directness and character of drawing we associate with child art. Where his detractors lost out was in their inability to respond to that elusive aestheticism, his absolute sureness of touch and his way of taking risks. By going against all the rules he was nevertheless completely right in the end. Nothing he did was ever banal, or slick, or even repetitive, and his instinct never let him down. But perhaps I'm being too solemn about François; essentially he was a creator of jokes and there's no difficulty in finding examples that are acceptable both in drawing and humour to most of us.

Another Frenchman, Jean-Jacques Sempé, has, I imagine, no detractors; no bemused and outraged readers rattle off letters of complaint about *his* work. He is very mainstream, very universal,

'I think if you let your hair down you'll be able to close your eyes.'

and very gifted. His ideas are locked firmly into the area which deals with human nature in all its strengths and frailties, but Sempé is no cynic – his attitude is warmly affectionate and any tartness underlying his ideas is effectively neutralised by the character of his drawing. He *likes* the people he draws, the houses they inhabit, the streets they walk, the country they travel. And it seems that he likes the act of drawing; not for him the graphic shorthand used by many cartoonists where locale and background are reduced to meagre symbols, but each room, each house, each stretch of landscape is observed as a real and unique place. Regrettably – and this is my personal view and one that Sempé would no doubt challenge – in the last couple of years or so he has found Art, which means that he is beginning to move away from the fluent rendering of people and places I have described above and is now deliberately coarsening his effects, deliberately formalising his subject matter. The reason for this, if in fact it is his reason, is easy to understand and I can sympathise with it.

In painting and to a large extent in graphics great facility is seldom admired; there is something suspect about it – it makes the job look too easy and because it looks easy it must therefore be slick and shallow and of baser quality. The primitive, on the other hand, with its guileless charm and awkwardness – and the amateur,

Two examples from Jean-Jacques Sempé. His ideas are generally set up within the drawing itself, so captions to a Sempé cartoon are rather rare. He is also adept at the multi-frame strip technique.

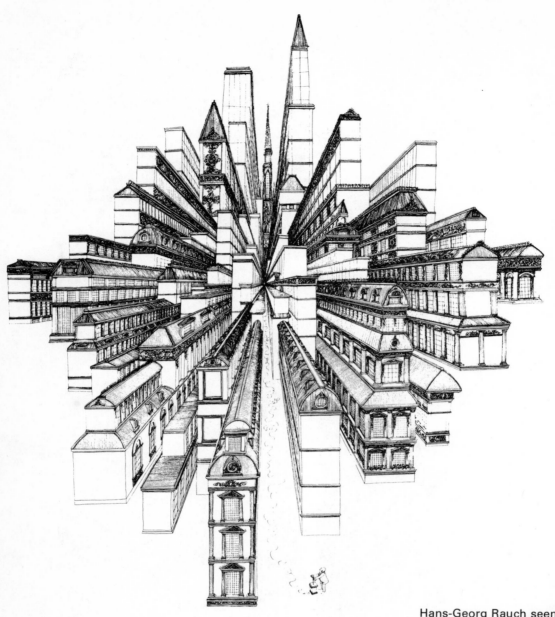

Hans-Georg Rauch seems to be fascinated by architecture – much of his work is concerned with the appearance of buildings. Above, he gives us an elegant visual pun, and on the right a comment on the decline of organised religion.

floundering about within tight boundaries of competence – are accorded a very different kind of assessment. The defects and the evident struggle somehow make the work more sincere and 'artistic' and therefore better – and only the completely assured would dare to contradict this. What makes the equation more difficult to condemn is the fact that some facile drawings *are* slick and shallow and some primitive drawings *are* extremely satisfying. (Thurber, whose cack-handed scribbles were absolutely right for him, has a lot to answer for.) I suspect that Sempé is moving towards the Thurberesque for the reasons I have indicated above; his wide popularity has been a barrier against his entry into the halls of high-camp graphics, his fluency of style a mark of his 'artistic' debility. His work has gathered wide acclaim – perhaps now he seeks the more rare approval of the intellectuals. Some clowns

reach out for Hamlet, some cartoonists apparently hanker after fine-art recognition.

François and Sempé – two Frenchmen. There is only one other major European cartoonist I'd like to include: Hans-Georg Rauch, a German. At first glance it might seem that Rauch's work was a good example of the artiness and pretentiousness of some European cartoonery. This assumption would be very wrong. True, his work is unlike the normal run of cartoons where the drawing is wheeled on merely as a vehicle to carry an idea; the emphasis with Rauch, who is first and foremost an artist, is firmly on the drawing element and through this he traces a very personal and quirky view of the world. There is seldom a 'joke' as such and never a caption. It is worth remembering that all drawing is in the way of being a conjuring trick: how otherwise do we convey the vastness of

the universe or a thought inside a man's head by means of a series
of dark marks on a flat surface? Rauch plays some very idiosyncratic tricks of his own and because these tricks are elegant and witty
and his draughtsmanship superb, there is nothing pretentious
about it. His drawings may assume much, and claim much, but
they do not fall short. Things, he tells us, are not always what they
appear to be, and even if they are there is a completely fresh
viewpoint from which they can be seen. We are his collaborators,
helpers called up from the audience – and we aren't fools, we can
read a drawing as well as the next man and can understand what
that tracery of lines represents. Rauch then jogs the table and we
see that the drawing means something more, or something less, or
even something different.

Two drawings by Ronald Searle from the series 'By Rocking-Chair Across America', in which he collaborated with the writer, Alex Atkinson. Searle is a master-draughtsman: very fluent, his pen an apparently natural extension to his hand. He has an unerring eye and memory for the detail that characterises each of the people he draws, and every line bears his inimitable signature. His range is wide: cartoons and political cartoons, illustration, caricature, graphic features, drawing for film. And if we add his prisoner-of-war drawings and his pictorial reportage of the Displaced Persons camps, he is arguably the foremost graphic artist of this century.

A trio of *New Yorker* stalwarts ploughing their own characteristic furrows: gentle black humour from Charles Addams, a Whitney Darrow dizzy blonde, and another skirmish in the battle of the sexes from James Thurber.

'What do you know! A sexagenarian turns out to be a guy in his sixties.'

Americana

'THEY have sinking spells. They can't ride on trains, or drive after dark, or live above the first floor of a building, or eat clams, or stay alone at night. They think that automobiles are coming up on the side-walk to get them, that gangsters are on their trail, that their apartments are being cased, and God knows what else.' Thus said Harold Ross, the legendary editor of *The New Yorker,* and he was talking about his cartoonists.

Ross, being Ross, is someone whose words we must take without the grain of salt; he being a non-writing, non-drawing, nothing-else-but editor and surrounded by the gang who *did*, was certainly in the best possible position to monitor the twitchy life style of his contributors.

On the surface, of course, those cartoonists were no different from the rest of us; moving in and out of 25 West 43rd Street they revealed none of the desperation that accompanied them through each day, none of the persecution mania that hung around their shoulders, none of the panic that visited them when the ideas failed to materialise. But Ross, yes Ross, knew. And through all this angst, this wringing of withers, what did these people produce? What did Whitney Darrow, George Price, W. Steig, Peter Arno, Perry Barlow, Modell, *et al* produce then? What do they produce now?

The facetious answer would be that they produced four drawings: a sugar daddy and a dewey blonde; two hoboes sitting on a

'All right, all right, try it that way! Go ahead and try it that way!'

'The strawberry magenta seems to be catching on.'

Many of Ed Fisher's cartoons have an historical setting through which he makes his humorous comments on the behaviour of today; in this one he abandons any historical parallel and instead opts for the classic salesman's view.

bench in Central Park; a drunk tête-à-tête with a barman; a man and wife getting into their car after a dinner-party. There would be captions, of course, many different captions, most of them sprinkled with three-syllabled words like nepotism, chimaera, and paradigm. Although grossly unfair, this travesty does point up our general impression of *New Yorker* cartoon humour: suave, sophisticated, literate, witty rather than funny, eastern-seaboard humour that chimes happily with the up-market ads. So perhaps there *is* a subliminal pattern lying underneath the apparent variety of subject matter and varied styles of drawing, perhaps it's fair to claim that at least. But it wasn't always so.

The New Yorker is over fifty years old now and some say it has sagged into a comfortable middle-aged spread; in the 'twenties and 'thirties it was very different. This was the aspirin age, the period of developing radio and the coming of the talkies and the animated cartoon film; there was zest, get-up-and-go, streamline. Ross's boys shook the old cartoon formula to pieces and kicked most of the bits away – where formerly it was static, congested and ponderously naturalistic they went after simplicity, directness and movement. They were after a humour that was essentially quick and visual. I would guess that nearly every cartoon produced today – in Britain or Europe or anywhere else – is in direct descent from *The New Yorker* humorous drawings of that period.

Before that time cartoons were word jokes with an illustration attached; they were quite often playlets bristling with elaborate stage directions hanging under a drawn tableau choked with detail. The reader expected this documentary style, this 'fine' accurate drawing, insisting that each picture should be a statement of facts with everything in its right place. This was the naturalistic drawing style of nineteenth- and twentieth-century pictorial humour which had little or no *expressive* dimension about it; the new humour of Ross's *New Yorker* demanded a new shorthand form of drawing which was heavily expressive – and expression is distortion, is stress, accent and vitality, is movement. Being autographic the drawings were deliberately simple and deliberately incorrect, which meant that they were full of character and could be funny *in themselves*. Through quickness of execution (or at least the illusion of quickness – a drawing could be done eight times before it was deemed to be 'right') they strove to attain suddenness of impact. Captions became shorter and shorter until on occasions they disappeared altogether leaving the picture itself to do all the work.

Demands were made on the reader, too – these streamlined ideas expected a streamlined response and the sluggards who were slow on the uptake were left behind. Not that there were many of those. The radio and the cinema had already quickened the pace of response and most readers found they could fill in the gaps themselves, could make the necessary connecting leaps without having every t crossed and every i dotted. It was quite a revolution.

Here in Britain we remained anchored to the old tradition but the new American style was so potent it was inevitable that we'd move in the same direction eventually, and that 'eventually' wasn't long in coming. By the mid-'thirties Paul Crum was bringing off those daring flights into the surreal (remember the hippos thinking it was Tuesday), a genre that can be traced back to nowhere else but *The New Yorker*. By then cross-hatching and the extended dialogue caption had already begun to look quaint even

One of Henry Martin's quiet quips on American office jargon and wisecrackery.

'Chief, I have good news and bad news. The bad news couldn't be worse and the good news couldn't be better. I also have some in-between news that couldn't be more so-so.'

'But Mr Deming, shouldn't we look for help before we huddle together for warmth?'

Peter Arno, the central rock of *The New Yorker* establishment but not, I admit, among those American cartoonists of particular appeal to me. The people who inhabit his cartoons tend to be roguish middle-aged executives on the loose, drawn in a firm, tubular manner. But he is stylish, and his influence can be readily seen elsewhere.

here. So if we feel that much of the humorous drawing in today's *New Yorker* is smart and urbane but stereotyped, it might be that we are making comparisons with its earlier days when it was way out in front and living dangerously.

What *does* remain distinctive and personal and very New Yorkerish is the character of the magazine's cover designs. The editorial attitude towards these seems to be cool and aloof but very much in control: it would appear that no concessions are made to the advertising department or the circulation department or even to the reader. The cover is very much an intimate dialogue between the artist and the editors and what results from this collaboration is a flavour you find nowhere else. It is totally admirable. As most of the cover artists (but not all) are established *New Yorker* cartoonists who have on this occasion slipped their leads and are no longer tethered to the Idea plus Black-and-White Drawing, maybe this release provides them with the stimulus to cast around and do their own thing. The results are quite often engagingly 'amateur' in the best sense of the word; the voice is always cultivated and well modulated – nothing shrill, nothing strident, the enjoyment of someone having a quiet afternoon off and left to his own devices.

There is also none of that Madison Avenue high camp about the covers, none of that high-quality gloss that trails in the wake of the graphics by Milton Glaser and his kind – it is a pleasant backwater with its own sedate atmosphere, a bit of Sunday painting, sometimes bizarre but never brittle. And in spite of this – *because* of this – these covers madden quite a lot of people who perhaps ought to know better, which is another thing in their favour.

Most of us who are familiar with *The New Yorker* have our own clutch of favourite cartoonists but there is a small group who for one reason or another command universal attention. These are artists who have climbed to the hall of fame, artists whose names immediately ring up a hard-edged image: Peter Arno, the king of the sugar daddies (and creator of that classic, 'Well, back to the drawing board'); Saul Steinberg, the intellectual juggler of symbols; Charles Addams, purveyor of chic sick; James Thurber, the word humorist who wandered into the wrong room and found he liked it there. If *The New Yorker* had given us no more than these it would have given us plenty.

And I'll bet they *all* ate clams.

Saul Steinberg does not permit examples of his work to appear in anthologies such as this one, so all I can offer is a parody which attempts to reflect some of his flavour. A lot of Steinberg lies below the surface.

A typically astringent encounter from Feiffer. He is not a *New Yorker* artist but is a New York one, his work coming first to our notice in *The Village Voice*.

There is a certain amount of fly-by-night humour around — fashionable stuff that meets the needs of the moment but after a few years looks extremely flat. Leslie Starke's cartoons, however, because they are firmly rooted in real human behaviour and because he took great pains to get them right, have the kind of quality that makes them stay. His drawings are always well composed, not only from the normal pictorial stand-point, but as the best possible method for projecting his ideas.

'My husband is the kind of man no one notices when he enters a room.'

'This is what I like – a nice empty pub. Pity the beer is so bloody awful.'

Into the Language

WORDS can be slippery things. Skewer them down to a hard definition and the next thing you know they've broken free and have bounced back into circulation dressed up in disguise and wearing a different hat. 'Contemporary' is such a turn-coat; it boldly appears even in the best circles as a synonym for 'modern' or 'present day'. Anybody who gives it the old meaning of 'belonging to the same time' runs the risk of being misunderstood or at least the accusation of being a bit of a pedant. 'Prestigious' also has a foot in two camps, on one side esteemed, on the other deceitful.

'Cartoon' is another word that has moved a tidy distance from its original technical meaning – so far, in fact, that on one well-publicised occasion when its old meaning was thrust back at the public at large that public could only giggle and look bewildered. That occasion was the day when a Leonardo da Vinci cartoon was offered for sale to the nation and it was put on display at the National Gallery. It was a largish drawing of a Madonna and Child and Leonardo had given it the full soupy treatment – plenty of shading and modelling. It was a cartoon because it was the preliminary drawing for a painting. Those droll comedians Peter Cook and Dudley Moore (in the roles of Pete and Dud) made much comical mileage out of that incident. ('Where's the caption, then?' 'What's funny about that?' Etcetera.) They were playing to the ignorance of a large audience who, up to then at least, had no idea that a cartoon was a preliminary drawing for a painting, a tapestry, or a mosaic; to them a cartoon ought to be a funny drawing and nothing more. What is interesting about this particular word-change is the fact that we can document the course through which

This drawing by John Leech was done in 1843 – the very first time that the word 'cartoon' was used in connection with a printed picture in a humour magazine. (Incidentally, he often 'signed' his work with a little pictograph showing a leech in a bottle; on this occasion he has written his name.)

CARTOON, No. 1.

SHADOW AND SUBSTANCE

*'Yes, **you** – 38 down and 247 across.'*

this change came about – a rare event, I should think, in the field of semantics and one worth recounting here.

In 1843 a large exhibition of cartoons was held consisting of designs for a number of frescoes intended for the walls of the Palace of Westminster which was then being built. The subject matter was rather lofty and allegorical and *Punch* seized the opportunity to publish its own 'Cartoons', not in parody form as the magazine would treat the subject today but as a radical satires which exposed some of the nastier social conditions of the time. They were drawn by John Leech. The first, labelled CARTOON No 1, bore the legend *The Poor ask for Bread and the Philanthropy of the State accords – an Exhibition.* In a similar attacking vein CARTOONS No 2 to 6 followed in the weeks after. Now at that time the drawings in *Punch* were known to the editorial staff as *cuts* (from being reproduced by wood-cuts, though strictly speaking the process was wood-engraving) and the full-page political drawing was always called The Big Cut. John Leech's CARTOONS were Big Cuts and after this series was published the Punch staff tended to refer to each subsequent political drawing as The Cartoon (a practice that continued until the regular full-page political cartoon was dropped a few years ago) and gradually this usage spilled over to include all the other joke drawings in the magazine. It is quite easy to see that from there this revised definition of the word *cartoon* spread out from the *Punch* offices to the public at large (Leech's CARTOONS had already registered strongly with many *Punch* readers) until today that definition is universally accepted as the predominant meaning. In fact it sometimes goes even further than that – there

David Langdon is one of the long-distance runners of cartooning; he started before the last War but it was his Air Force jokes which established his name in the public mind. Since that time he has regularly produced a score of topical ideas each week – the more oblique ones aimed at *Punch*, the broader approach for the *Sunday Mirror*. From these *Punch* selects two, the *Sunday Mirror* four. The example shown here is one of his 'non topicals'.

are people who now refer to caricatures as a cartoon, though these are two kinds of drawings which the practitioner always keeps severely apart.

Drawing-board Metaphors

The world of cartooning has had its effects on our language in other ways, too, offering us new metaphors and allusions and even clichés. Some of these have been reduced to a scrappy shorthand on the assumption that the original source and its implications are common knowledge. A good example would be the Curate's Egg – journalists and politicians need only to suggest that this plan or that proposition is 'like the Curate's Egg' and everybody knows that it is therefore 'good in parts'. Or in other words, partly acceptable, partly not. The du Maurier cartoon which originated this

TRUE HUMILITY

Right Reverend Host: "I'm afraid you've got a bad egg, Mr. Jones!"
The Curate: "Oh no, my Lord, I assure you! Parts of it are excellent!"

phrase was quite a funny one – not only at the time but now, too – saying much more about the relationships between people and between castes than would first seem obvious. It is possibly because of these extra layers that the cartoon was so often quoted and thus entered the language.

Bruce Bairnsfather's 'If you knows of a better 'ole, go to it,' hasn't quite the wide currency of that curate's egg but it still appears from time to time as a quick way of saying that it is probably best to stay and face out the problems here and now because things are just as bad everywhere else. Bairnsfather's 'Old Bill' soldier peering out of a shell hole during a Somme bombardment is perhaps a dim memory even for those who use his phrase but the drawing does get a new lease of life from the frequent parodies favoured by political cartoonists. I suspect that Old Bill and his 'better 'ole' will be around quite a while yet.

And it's not just particular cartoons but the names of particular cartoonists which enter the language by the back door. Few British

Captured Burglar: *'Just my luck! I spends six munce makin' friends wiv the dorg, an' then I goes an' treads on the perishin' cat.'*

people will be puzzled when a contraption or even an arrangement is described as 'very Heath Robinson'; what they mean is a bizarre and shaky improvisation. Roland Emett gave his name to the adjective 'Emettish' – again this is applied to any collection of grotesque improvised machinery. And when we hear of a 'St Trinian's' schoolgirl or a 'Thelwell' pony, we know exactly what that girl and that pony are like.

There is another phrase in common use which has been extracted from the caption to another old Victorian cartoon in *Punch* but this time we have the tail but not the body. *Collapse of stout party* is a phrase which has come to encapsulate that whole genre of Victorian humorous art where the captions are extended dialogue in playlet form, thick with stage directions and loaded with a mass of extraneous information. *Collapse of stout party* was the final pay-off in parentheses; now it serves us again in headings and titles to articles, in features and books devoted to any form of Victoriana. Curiously enough, even with the help of the *Punch*

The Victorian middle class often felt that the lower orders were rather comical. Browse through the bound volumes of *Punch* for that period and you will battle through a thicket of cartoon captions in dialects of stupifying complexity. Bert Thomas carried on this mainstream tradition between the wars and the reason why his drawings are exceptional is because he portrayed his characters with a deadly accuracy and liveliness. Look at the example above – this is certainly drawing *con brio*, a natural descendant from Phil May's bravura style.

Is this 1931 drawing by J.H. Dowd really a cartoon? It was published as such, yet it is more heavily charged with pathos than with any humour. It features the lower orders again, this time with sympathy but very close to sentimentality.

Hospital Patient (one of large family in poor district, given a glass of milk): 'HOW FAR DOWN CAN I DRINK?'

THE PLEASURE SEEKERS

By Scarfe

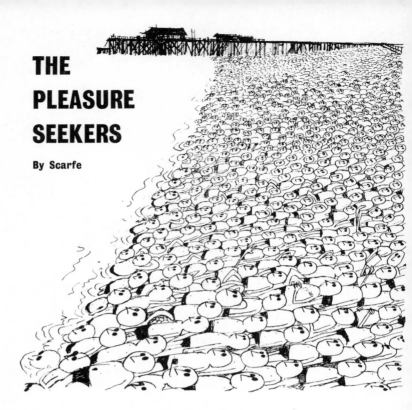

In the 'sixties Gerald Scarfe attracted some notoriety when he appointed himself as the scourge of mankind. He looked at his fellow men (and women) and despised what he saw. The corrective, he felt, was Shock, and the meat cleaver was his administering tool. Goya and Gillray were much in his mouth. Here is an early satirical feature when he was limbering up for the main attack; those spilled entrails were to come later. He is an excellent draughtsman and fine caricaturist though lately there are signs that he has lost a certain amount of interest.

Librarian, I have not been able to track down the cartoon to which it was attached. There is always the possibility that it derives from a more recent spoof, but somehow it has the ring of parody about it – and there is acceptable evidence that it started out as 'Collapse of Elderly Gentleman' and got mangled on the way.

A more useful and more used phrase is, 'Well, back to the drawing-board,' which was originally a caption to a Peter Arno full-page drawing in *The New Yorker,* spoken by a quite unworried man with a roll of technical drawings under his arm as he watched an aeroplane disintegrating on the ground. It's a fair chance that any evidence of failure will now spring that caption into the conversation. 'Take me to your leader' is another heavily used phrase but this example has a more involved history. I suppose initially it harked back to those adventure stories cast in the Rider Haggard mould and it was the cartoonist's back-reference to this source that gave it a fresh lease of life in the 1950s when Alex Graham produced the very first Martian/Flying saucer cartoon with this caption. I hope you won't think me too perverse when I reveal that Graham's caption was not 'Take me to your leader', but 'Take us to

your President'. His drawing, published in *The New Yorker,* showed a flying-saucer in a field and two bug-eyed Martians talking to a horse. I cannot guess how many variations this produced but on all of them the caption used *leader* instead of *President,* perhaps to reach a wider audience. Robot Martians said it to petrol pumps, gnomic Martians said it to Harold Macmillan on a grouse moor (he *was* the British leader at that time – a neat flick of satire from Smilby) and yet other Martians rang the bell at Franz Schubert's door and asked to be taken to his *lieder.* The phrase appeared in advertisements, in chat shows, in drama scripts. It had a very good run for its money, though I'm not sure how Graham feels about fathering such a brood.

In cartoon terms I suppose 'Take me to your leader' could be called a restricted cliché; the idea became common property and there was a quick rush by cartoonists to get in with their own variations because there was obviously a limit to what could be done – unlike the standard cartoon clichés, some of which simply refuse to fade away. Egyptian hieroglyphics, Noah's Ark, the Trojan horse, vikings, elephants, knights in armour, L-drivers,

'My compliments to the chef.'

psychiatrists, yogis, harems, computers, heaven (people in night-shirts on clouds), and hell (naked people dancing through the flames) promise to be with us for a long time. And, of course, the daddy of them all, the Desert Island – for just when you believe that absolutely nothing new can be said about a desert island someone comes up with proof that there can. More recently we've had clichés made out of abandoned cars, factory farming, pollution, package holidays, progressive education. At the turn of the century comic papers had a regular sprinkling of cockney charladies, ignorant Irishmen, silly-ass aristocrats, sarcastic Scottish gillies, chaotic fox-hunting. There was even a cliché made out of something that as far as I know does not exist – the Complaints counter. I used to think it an American phenomenon until Americans told me no, they thought it was an English one. And when you think about it the notion of a department store admitting at the outset that there are bound to be complaints is just bad commercial psychology. I suspect that in the beginning a cartoonist thought of an idea about a customer wishing to complain about some purchase, and the most direct way to illustrate that situation was to introduce a special counter with a COMPLAINTS notice above it. From that point onwards through all the new variations those Complaints counters became very real.

Perhaps this reliance on recurring subject matter does suggest that the cartoonist's inventiveness is a restricted and even an incestuous one. This is true, but only up to a point – an existing cartoon does tend to trigger off further variations. It also has an added merit (or fault, if you are disposed that way): it presents other cartoonists with a subject to think around, a subject that has already been demonstrated as a valid one for humorous ideas. Even so, most practitioners, certainly in the higher echelons, prefer to steer clear of these cliché subjects and look for their material within their own particular interests and the life they observe going on around them.

'My compliments to the Chef' (and 'This is my husband's little den', and 'Take me to your leader') is a cliché caption that challenges cartoonists to prise out yet another variation. Here, Smilby and Raymonde have met that challenge quite neatly.

'My compliments to the reconstitutor.'

124

'Be reasonbale, guv – where can I find the Chief Rabbi on Early Closing Day?'

So there it is. Humorous art, cartooning, joke-drawing – call it what you will – a curious way to earn a living some would say. But I hope that these meanderings through and around and across the art of pictorial humour have been able to give some notion of what it's like on the other side of the drawing board, the other side of the rejection slip. Very occasionally, of course, it is possible for the humorous artist to lose and win at the same time.

In my early days of cartooning, my father-in-law once proclaimed that the cartoon I had in the current issue of *Punch* was the best, the funniest I had produced to date. This was gratifying because he was a hard-headed engineer and not given to casting fulsome praise around the place. The trouble was I had no cartoon in that particular issue of *Punch*. So I probed for more details which got the pages turning until they finally stopped at the book reviews. In those days the main review had a little single-column decoration set in the middle of it, something to add a bit of 'colour' to the page, and the theme of the drawing was anchored firmly to the text. I had done the illustration that week.

Now what possible humorous idea he had discovered within that drawing was something I felt it best to leave alone, but somehow he had. In plays, in books, people see great profundities never intended by the playwright or the author; if they see comedy where none was intended then we should not be too unhappy about that – after all, it quite often goes the other way. But this anecdote reinforces that premise I suggested earlier: humour lies in the eye of the beholder and not necessarily anywhere else.

A similar incident also occurred some years ago, at a time when a certain cartoonist had the job of filling the same space each week on the final page of a magazine. Every Tuesday his cartoon arrived and every Tuesday the art editor approved it and sent it on its way to the blockmaker. One Tuesday the idea failed to get this approval. The art editor put it in his OUT tray with *Sorry, not this one, I'm afraid* scribbled at the bottom of the drawing. Now the artist was so

Another cliché, this time in the situation. There have been scores of would-be suicides from building ledges but Dickinson proves that the subject is not yet exhausted.

There have been few women cartoonists and Anton was perhaps the most distinguished of them. She specialised in extremely tall, doe-eyed women, and her humour was nearly always the quiet, 'recognition' type.

'Would it be all right to dilute it with water to begin with?'

125

sure of getting regular approval he had fallen into the habit of pencilling the line-block measurement underneath his cartoon – a small task that normally lies within the art editor's domain. It was after the secretary had collected this rejected drawing that things started to go wrong. Instead of sending it back to the artist she booked it out in the usual way and dispatched it to the printer. The cartoon was now locked into the system. When the next issue of the magazine came out the final page featured this drawing, but whereas the artist had given it no caption the published version had acquired one: 'Sorry, not this one, I'm afraid'.

It is a common experience in drama circles that all kinds of mis-cues and other disasters can batter a performance and yet escape the notice of the audience, or at the worst a section in the front stalls might be aware of an occasional ripple disturbing the smooth flow of the play. A similar relationship may stand between the producers of a magazine and its readership, and perhaps this had some bearing on reader response to this strange hybrid cartoon. Also, by a lucky fall of the dice, this bogus caption – helped by a stretched imagination – could be made to fit the drawing subject. It was puzzling, as many cartoons can be, but not too outlandish. Now if a reader of *Punch* misses the point of a cartoon he will more than likely ring up to find out what it was, because no one cares to be fenced off from a joke. In the case I have just outlined I understand that no reader did this. Perhaps it was universally accepted as an ultra-subtle cartoon or an extra-zany one. Perhaps that accidental cartoon still lives with some readers and is cherished by them as a piece of high quality surrealism on a par with Paul Crum's hippos. It's an attractive thought. It also underlines the sub-text that I hope has been running through all I've written so far: it is really not possible to define humour. G. K. Chesterton went even further. He said, 'It would commonly be regarded as a deficiency in humour to search for a definition of humour.'

'Other men just **sing** in the bath.'

Humble Recognition Humour often skirts very close to being just plain ordinary; similarly, David Myers' own particular brand of humour (a very personal one) can be hilariously nonsensical or just plain silly, depending on who is looking at it. Is the Piano-in-Bath drawing funny or is it silly? The Dentist and the Sex Shop cartoons are slightly different – they have their own watertight logic and are much closer to real human behaviour. But what all Myers' cartoons do have is an extremely comic style of drawing. If those marching dogs cannot raise a smile then I'm afraid there is no hope for you.

'Phew, that was quite a day.'

'Frankly, I feel he over-disciplines his animals.'

A burr that scratches many cartoonists is the worry that they will dry up and produce no more ideas, and it is quite true that occasionally a humorist of talent will suddenly drop out from the running. Others are marathon men who run and run. Such a stayer is J.W. Taylor, a schoolmaster (now retired) who sold his first cartoon in 1937 and who has kept up a constant flow of high quality ideas ever since. His humour has a cerebral cast to it and he does not belittle his readers by assuming that they cannot make the mental jumps necessary for the appreciation of his work. J.W. Taylor is a name largely unsung in the field of cartooning mainly because he has failed to concentrate on single themes such as music or monks or motoring, but has thrown his net very much wider. These two examples are vintage Taylor, I believe: Edward DeBono's conception of Lateral Thinking here turned into a new alignment. Also re-aligned is a piece of motoring jargon.

'I just want something to get me from A to B and back without arousing A's suspicions.'